Highly Irregular

HIGHLY Irregular

WHY TOUGH, THROUGH, AND DOUGH DON'T RHYME—

AND OTHER ODDITIES OF THE ENGLISH LANGUAGE

ARIKA OKRENT

ILLUSTRATED BY

SEAN O'NEILL

OXFORD
UNIVERSITY PRESS

OXFORD
UNIVERSITY PRESS

Oxford University Press is a department of the University of Oxford. It furthers the University's objective of excellence in research, scholarship, and education by publishing worldwide. Oxford is a registered trade mark of Oxford University Press in the UK and certain other countries.

Published in the United States of America by Oxford University Press
198 Madison Avenue, New York, NY 10016, United States of America.

© Arika Okrent 2021

Library of Congress Cataloging-in-Publication Data
Names: Okrent, Arika, author.
Title: Highly irregular : why tough, through, and dough don't rhyme—and other oddities of the English language / Arika Okrent ; Illustrations by Sean O'Neill.
Description: New York : Oxford University Press, 2021. |
Includes bibliographical references and index.
Identifiers: LCCN 2021004585 (print) | LCCN 2021004586 (ebook) |
ISBN 9780197539408 (hardback) | ISBN 9780197539422 (epub)
Subjects: LCSH: English language—Orthography and spelling—History. |
English language—Pronunciation.
Classification: LCC PE1141 .O35 2021 (print) | LCC PE1141 (ebook) |
DDC 421/.52—dc23
LC record available at https://lccn.loc.gov/2021004585
LC ebook record available at https://lccn.loc.gov/2021004586

DOI: 10.1093/oso/9780197539408.001.0001

3 5 7 9 8 6 4

Printed by Sheridan Books, Inc., United States of America

table of contents

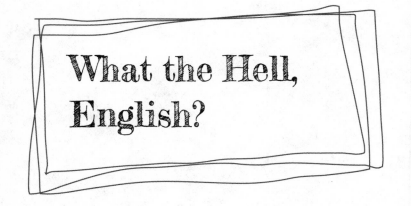

What the Hell, English?

Dearest creature in creation
Studying English pronunciation,
    I will teach you in my verse
    Sounds like corpse, corps, horse and worse.
I will keep you, Susy, busy,
Make your head with heat grow dizzy;
    Tear in eye, your dress you'll tear;
    Queer, fair seer, hear my prayer.
Pray, console your loving poet,
Make my coat look new, dear, sew it!
    Just compare heart, hear and heard,
    Dies and diet, lord and word.

So begins the poem "The Chaos," which the Simplified Spelling Society called "an indictment of the chaos of English spelling," or, more flamboyantly, a "compendium of cacography." It was printed in the society's summer newsletter in 1986 and went on for 246 lines. It came with a specific request: "Can any reader name the author or supply any further details about the poem?"

Before landing with the editor of the newsletter, the poem had passed through many hands. It was rumored to have been discovered in a girls' high school in Germany at the end of World War II. Retyped and mimeographed copies of slightly different versions had made their way around Europe. There were stories from students of English in various countries who recalled their professors using it in class to broach, in a lighthearted way, the frustrating challenge of figuring out how to match sound and spelling in the language.

The origin of the poem was eventually tracked down, and in 1994 the Simplified Spelling Society issued an update. The author was a Dutch writer named Gerard Nolst Trenité. The poem was first published in 1920 in an appendix to the fourth edition of his book *Drop Your Foreign Accent: engelsche uitspraakoefeningen.* The Dutch subtitle translates to "a guide to English pronunciation," but Nolst Trenité clarified that it was "not a guide" but "an exercise book . . . less like a drill-master, who teaches you how to perform your feats, than like a set of gymnastic apparatus on which you have to perform them yourself—vocal gymnastics."

The main apparatus was verse, in which "rhythm and rhyme may act as fly-wheels, strengthening and equalizing the movement of the vocal organs." The poems he supplied were easy to commit to memory, and, he suggested, "Having chosen those which contain your special stumbling-blocks, you may conveniently practice them during a lonely walk, sitting all by yourself in a railway carriage, etc."

He should know. After all, he had had to do the work to learn to produce it himself. Born in Utrecht in 1870, he learned English (among other languages) the hard way, at school. After university, he spent two years in San Francisco, where he worked as a tutor for the children of a Dutch family. But otherwise, aside from a short stint teaching English and French in the Dutch East Indies, he spent the rest of his life in the Netherlands, in Haarlem, at the same address.

Most of Nolst Trenité's career was spent not in explaining the challenging intricacies of English but in nitpicking defense of his own native language. For more than thirty years he had a column in the *Groene Amsterdammer* where, writing under the name Charivarius, he scolded, berated, teased, and criticized his fellow countrymen for their sloppy and annoying language habits.

Charivarius had a long list of favorite annoyances: too much capitalization in titles; the overuse of the word *nauwelijks* (hardly); Germanisms, such as the use of *slagroom* for whipped cream instead of the pure Dutch *geklopte room*. He railed against pleonasms like "fierce fire" (fire is already fierce!) and "useless waste" (waste is already understood to be useless!) and came up with his own labels for his favorite peeves. *Fnaffers* and *fnuiters* were those who used *vanaf* and *vanuit* (from off, from out) for what he decreed should be simply *van* (from).

Many of these "errors" are fully accepted in Dutch now, and some of them may have only ever bothered Charivarius to begin with.

Drop Your Foreign Accent went through seven editions during Nolst Trenité's lifetime (and four more after his 1946 death). "The Chaos" nearly doubled in length over that time, as Nolst Trenité thought of more and more English spelling inconsistencies to add to it. As the poem grew, so did the force of its comic absurdity. In one book of his collected verses, he introduced it with the line "May it spread fear and dismay."

The final lines of the poem itself read:

Finally: which rhymes with *enough,*
Though, through, plough, cough, hough, or *tough?*
Hiccough has the sound of 'sup' . . .
My advice is—give it up!

But of course he didn't really want the reader to give up on English. He ends the introduction to *Drop Your Foreign Accent* with a notification that the appendix includes a "small collection of phonetical paradoxes" in verse form and that "the last line contains an advice; my advice is—don't take it."

Nolst Trenité saw that the Dutch language had its own inconsistencies too. One poem called "Taal-Rijm" (Language rhyme) was "dedicated to the foreigner who learns Dutch." He points out, for example, that while the plural of *bal* (ball) is *ballen*, the plural of *dal* (valley) is not *dallen*. Collected all together, these types of irregularities do not reach nearly the same level of absurdity or of inspiring "fear and dismay" as those in "The Chaos." After all, they are common in many other languages, including English (the plural of *box* is not *boxen*).

It is notable that when he tries to incorporate some of the type of spelling irregularities of his English hit into his poem on Dutch, it's a really effortful stretch. He comes up with only one or two place names (the city of Gorinchem is pronounced 'gorkum') and the pair *meester* (starfish) and *zeester* (sister), which don't quite fully rhyme, but only because they have slightly different stress patterns. While "The Chaos" ends with full-throated ironic drama ("My advice is—give it up!") "Taal-Rijm" peters out with a gentle shrug: "Dutch is not so easy either."

Nolst Trenité could not make anything comparable to "The Chaos" for Dutch because Dutch doesn't have anything like the English spelling problem. No other European language does. French has its share of silent letters and alternate ways of spelling the same sound, but it is far more systematic. All languages have their infelicities and awkward bits, but English has its own special kind of weirdness. It can be hard to see from the inside. English speakers are well aware of the oddness of spellings like *colonel* or *hors d'oeuvres*, but it takes an outsider like a foreigner trying to learn the language or a Nolst Trenité trying to teach it to see that *sew* and *new* should rhyme but don't.

Not only did Nolst Trenité have an outsider's perspective, but he had the language pedant's perspective. His complaints about the way his fellow citizens butchered the Dutch language were different from his complaints about English, but they came from the same expectation that language should be a logical, orderly system.

This is an expectation which most of us share to a degree. It's why we find a poem like "The Chaos" funny. It says, "Behold the utter lack of systematicity in this system!" If we didn't think there was supposed to be a system, the joke would be meaningless. And we know, implicitly, that there is a system, despite all the messy exceptions. That is why, if we come across an unfamiliar word like *frew*, we will not be overcome with confusion and uncertainty, but simply rhyme it with *new*. It's why we can come up with a spelling to make ourselves understood, even if we get it wrong, as children often do. There are patterns and regularities to exploit. Those patterns and regularities are rules.

However, the patterns are often overshadowed by what looks like randomness, and there are irregularities everywhere, not just in the spelling system. At every level of language, from spelling to vocabulary to grammar to word order to meaning, there are violations of harmony and order.

These violations might be more obvious to non-English speakers trying to learn it, but if English is your native language, you are still often forced to confront them. A colleague who has learned English as a second language asks you why it's wrong to say "Let's go them over" when "Let's look them over" is fine, and you find yourself sinking in logical quicksand as you try to come up with an answer. A child asks you why there's an *l* in *could*, and you throw up your hands and say, "English is just weird." But it's not the case that English is *just* weird. It's weird in specific ways for specific reasons. It's not utterly unexplainable chaos. It's just highly irregular.

Highly Irregular can be read in two different, complementary ways. It is a collection of answers to questions about English, some familiar (How does an exception prove a rule? Why do noses run and feet smell?) and some that may never have occurred to you before (How come we say *how come*? Why isn't *of* spelled with a *v*?). These can be casually browsed in any order.

At the same time, if read from start to finish, it will present a deeper story, a history of English that explores the tension between logic and habit in language development. Language is always being pulled in two directions. It is infinitely generative, allowing us to draw from a limited set of units, sounds, words, idioms, and phrases to create sentences that have never been spoken before, meanings that have never been expressed before, texts that have never been written before. It is also conservative, a cultural tradition that we pass from person to person, embedded in everyday habits that are reinforced by social pressure, institutional customs, and constant repetition.

In most cases, the explanation for why things are the way they are is a story about the way they were and why people either changed them or kept them frozen while the world changed around them. The individual articles are organized into five sections, and if you read just the introduction to each of these sections, you get a nice, compact history of English.

Before diving into that history, we'll take a brief tour of the type of weirdness this book is about. When I told people I was writing about the weirdness of English, the places where it didn't seem to conform to a system or even to logic, they often had suggestions for questions I could address, such as "Why do people confuse *loose* and *lose*?" or "Why do some people say 'This needs washed'?" The assumption was that the place to look for unsystematic or illogical English was in mistakes or deviations from the correct standard.

But one doesn't need to turn to nonstandard English to find the flaws, as anyone who has studied English as a foreign language can tell you. The types of questions I will deal with here are part of fully accepted, unquestionably correct, standard English. The language is shot through with absurdity, and I will begin in this section with a selection of questions that illustrate how the weirdness permeates all levels, from pronunciation and spelling (Why is *y* a "sometimes" vowel? What is the deal with the word *colonel*?)

to word meaning and sentence structure (Why do we order a *large* drink and not a *big* one? Why do we drive on a parkway and park on a driveway? What the hell is with *What the hell?*).

Then we move on to the (good-natured! jocular!) question of who is to blame for this mess. First, we can blame the barbarians (section 2), who gave us the old, fossil layers of the language that continue to make the surface bumpy. Then, we can blame the French (section 3) for centuries of linguistic rule, but only in some areas and not others, fracturing our vocabulary and writing system. Then we can blame the printing press (section 4) for ironing in weird wrinkles that might have otherwise smoothed themselves out. And then we can blame the snobs (section 5) for top-down decisions made from inconsistent personal gripes.

Though these sections are arranged in general historical order, the boundaries from one era to the next are porous. Answers are assigned to one section, even when they result from the accumulation of many types of blame. And the final section, "Blame Ourselves" (section 6), describes not the final stage of the history of English but one that has been there all along. Everything that happens to language happens because of us humans and the way we are.

No engineer would purposefully design a language to be this disorderly. But language is not the product of engineering. It is the product of evolution, and the faults of English are similar to those that can be found in our bodies. Why do we have an appendix? Why are we so prone to back pain? Why do we love unhealthy food? Some biological adaptations help us at one point but hurt us later. Some changes stick around for no reason at all. The process of evolution does not itself have a goal, but it makes us what we are. Some strengths become weaknesses; some useful parts become useless.

The *gh* in English spelling is like our appendix. It used to have a function but now dangles there mutely, except when it flares up to cause problems for people learning to spell. Irregular verbs are our lower back pain, a product of adjusting an old skeletal structure to a new way of getting around. Figurative *literally* is a big, juicy cheeseburger, so tempting even when we know the experts are telling us it's no good.

Despite the parallels, when it comes to language, the evolution metaphor can only go so far. In the past thousand years, our bodies have hardly changed at all, while our languages have become unrecognizable. Language is a social institution, and the path it takes is determined not by the transmission of genes from one generation to the next but by the transmission of utterances from one person to the next. We have a role, both as individuals and as groups, in determining what language will do. And yet, try as we might, we can't willfully control it. We make the rules, but not by actively deciding what they should be. If we did, they'd be a lot less messy.

The Colonel of Truth

What Is the Deal with the Word *Colonel*?

One of the worst offenders in a crowded field of unbelievable English spellings is *colonel*, pronounced 'kernel.' Where do we get that 'r' sound from? Why are there silent 'o's? What the heck is going on with this word? How can it be so shamelessly nonsensical?

CHOMP CHOMP

POP CORN

There's plenty of blame to go around for this one, but it starts with the French. They borrowed the word from the Italians, making a bit of a change in the process, and we borrowed it from the French. Much of the English vocabulary of warfare comes to us this way, from Italian through French—words like *cavalry, infantry, citadel, battalion, brigade, corporal*, and also *colonel*. When one language borrows from another, the words get adapted to fit the new language. Italian *cavalleria* became French *cavalerie* became English *calvary*. *Infanteria* became *infanterie* became *infantry*.

But when the French borrowed *colonnello* from the Italians, they changed it to *coronel*.

Why did they do that? It wasn't just a random mistake. It came through a very common process called dissimilation. When two instances of the same sound occur close to each other in a word, people tend to change one of the instances to something else or drop it altogether. Think of the words *prerogative* or *surprise*. Most of the time English speakers pronounce these without the first *r*.

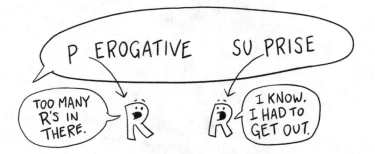

The 'l' and 'r' sounds are frequent players in the dissimilation game, whether by switching places or dropping out. Because of this, Latin developed two endings to make a noun into an adjective, *-alis* or *-aris*, depending on whether there were other 'l's close by in the root. From *vita* (life), we get *vit-alis* (vital), "pertaining to life." From *tempus* (time), we get *tempor-alis* (temporal), "pertaining to time." But the adjectives from *populus* (the people) and *regula* (rule) were *popul-aris* and *regul-aris*. *Populalis* and *regulalis* were just too *l*-ful for Latin.

Some words were just too *r*-ful for other languages. The classical Latin word *peregrinus* (pilgrim) became *pelegrinus* in late Latin and then *pellegrino* in Italian and *pelerin* in French, and this version with the *l* is what we based *pilgrim* on. When we speak of the peregrine falcon, however, we go with the classical *peregrinus*-based form. It's not that people can't say words with too many *r*'s or *l*'s too close to each other; it's just very common and unsurprising for languages to switch things up in these cases.

Other *r*-to-*l* switches resulted in English *purple* and *marble* (from *pupure* and *marbre*). *Arbor* and *miraculum* became *arbol* and *milagro* in Spanish. It happens.

Which is to say the French recasting of *colonnello* as *coronel* is totally normal and no big deal. We borrowed it with the *coronel* spelling and three-syllable pronunciation ('co-ro-nel') in the mid-1500s, but over time the pronunciation got reduced to 'kernel.' This is also pretty normal and expected. Whole syllables have disappeared from words like *chocolate* ('choklit'), *vegetable* ('vegtible'), *favorite* ('favrit'), and many others.

What's not normal and expected is the way we ended up with the spelling *colonel*. In the late sixteenth century scholars started producing English translations of Italian military treatises. Under the influence of the originals, where they kept seeing *colonnello*, scholarly types started spelling it *colonel* instead of *coronel*. This version had the shine of the more literary, etymologically correct choice. The French, also reading these Italian works, started writing *colonel* as well.

After some back and forth, by 1650 the spelling had standardized to the *l* version. But the French, who had introduced the whole *r* version in the first place, adjusted their pronunciation to the new spelling and said 'co-lo-nel.' And while many English speakers also pronounced it with the *l*, enough people just kept on pronouncing it the 'kernel' way. In the 1700s pronouncing dictionaries listed the *colonel* spelling with the 'kernel' pronunciation.

The ultimate resolution, Italian-style *l* spelling with French-style *r* pronunciation (which the French no longer themselves used), did not go unremarked upon for its absurdity. It became a popular nineteenth-century joke, in limericks such as this:

> There was a brave soldier, a Colonel,
> Who swore in a way most infolonel;
> But he never once thought
> As a Christian man ought
> He imperiled his own life etolonel.

Colonel snuck in through successive waves of borrowing and the establishment of habits that became hard to break. The early French version spread the pronunciation; the later Italian-inspired version spread the spelling among a certain class of people—those who do a lot of writing and so spread the standards for writing (see "Blame the Snobs"). But it's harder to change how things are spoken. Spoken 'col'nel' made an appearance, but simply couldn't catch on.

And so we're left with the ridiculous contradiction of *colonel*. So ridiculous it's become almost a point of pride. *Colonel* can be 'kernel' if we say so. That's the stubborn defiance of English.

Fairweather Vowels

Why Is *Y* a Sometimes Vowel?

First we learn to speak, then we learn to write. Somewhere in between, we learn to recite the alphabet. We train it into our consciousness through repetition, memorization, and a special song. Once we've got the alphabet down, we learn about an important subset of the alphabet, the vowels, and it has its own memorization routine to go with it—a chant that goes like this: *a, e, i, o, u* . . . and sometimes *y*.

Sometimes? There were none of these provisional "sometimes" members in the alphabet song. The letters all seemed to know they were letters. Why is *y* so unsure if it's a vowel or a consonant? Can't it just decide what it is? Why is *y* a "sometimes" vowel?

Understanding the why of *y* involves a very important and often overlooked fact. Writing is not the same thing as speech.

If I ask you what letter a word starts with, you know that I am asking about the written form of the word, not the spoken form. If

I ask "What letter does *psychology* start with" the answer is *p*, even though, as spoken, it starts with an 's' sound.

If I ask you "What vowel does *aunt* start with" there are two ways to answer, depending on whether we're talking about the written form or the spoken. For the written form the answer is simple: *a*. For the spoken form, it's complicated: "an 'a' sound like in *cat*" or "an 'ah' sound like in *father*" or "an 'aw' sound like in *saw*." *Vowel* can mean two different things, a written symbol or a sound.

It's difficult to write about spoken vowels in a clear and precise way. I have no idea what dialect you, the reader, speak or how you actually pronounce *cat*, *father*, or *saw*. Linguists use special symbols from something called the International Phonetic Alphabet when discussing specific sounds. The three vowel sounds in *aunt* mentioned above would be /æ/, /ɑ/, and /ɔ/. Unfortunately, most people don't learn to use that alphabet, so we have to resort to approximations like 'aw' or descriptions like "as in *saw*." Our regular alphabet is not built to handle the sounds of English very well.

While we casually refer to letters, which are written symbols, as vowels or consonants, the concepts of vowel and consonant properly belong to the domain of speech. In general terms, a consonant is a speech sound formed by some kind of constriction or impeding of air flow through the vocal tract, and a vowel lets the air flow freely through.

In English, we have twenty-one *written* letters (if you count *y*) that we call consonants. But if we're talking about speech, there are twenty-five or so. How does that work? Well, some consonants don't get their own letters. 'Sh' is a single consonant sound. We just reuse two other letters in order to spell it.

There are twelve or sixteen or maybe even twenty vowels in English, depending on your dialect. There's *a* as in *cat* or *father*, *e* as in *be* or *bed*, *i* as in *sir* or *big*, *o* as in *soap* or *look*, and *u* as in *sum* or *true*. We haven't even gotten to the vowel sounds in *house* or *time* or *say*. And if you come from New York or Scotland or Texas, these descriptions will work differently for you.

So as mentioned before, if, when it comes to spoken language, consonants constrict while vowels let the air flow freely through, then what kind of sound does *y* represent? It can stand for either type. In *yes*, *y* is representing a consonant, and in *gym* it is representing a vowel.

In fact, due to the imperfect match between writing and speech, there are other "sometimes" vowels: *w* is a consonant in *we* and part of a diphthong vowel in *now*. *H* is a consonant in *hat*, but what is it in *ah*? It's part of the representation of a different vowel sound; compare the phrase *a man* with *ah, man*. If we look hard enough, we can even find examples of "sometimes" consonants. What sound does the *o* represent in *one*? What sound does the *u* represent in *united*? They are consonant + vowel combinations 'wuh' and 'yu.'

We don't bother to add the "sometimes" clause for letters other than *y* because in practical terms *y* is the only one that really needs that qualification. It's the one that swings between vowel and consonant the most. It represents a consonant in common words like *you, year, yet*, and *beyond*. It represents a vowel at the end of all kinds of words (*my, by, fly, merry, curry, study*) and suffixes that attach to words (*lemon-y, understanding-ly*). But the reason we probably learn the "sometimes" clause when we learn to read is because *y* also represents a vowel in the *middle* of a bunch of words that have etymological origins in Greek (*syllable, system, cycle, type, hyper, lyrics, gym*). That's a position where in the rest of the language we'd usually find an *a, e, i, o*, or *u*. They are spelled that way because they had the Greek letter ypsilon in that position.

A, e, i, o, u, and sometimes *y* is not a bad rule of thumb. Most of the time a spoken vowel will be represented by one of those written forms. But it's worth remembering that letters are not speech sounds. They are lines on a page that nudge us, quite imperfectly, toward the sounds of the things we say.

Hey Large Spender

Why Do We Order a *Large* Drink and Not a *Big* One?

Big and *large* mean the same thing, right? If you live in a big town, you live in a large town. A big factory is a large factory. The biggest box of paper clips is the largest box of paper clips.

But there are many, many examples where *big* and *large* cannot be swapped for each other without changing the sense in some way. *Large* can make a phrase sound more formal or stuffy, even when it expresses the same sense of size. It would be strange to tell a toddler "Look at that large doggie!" or "I have a large present for you!" *Big* is more common and relaxed in everyday language.

It would also be strange to tell a toddler "What a large boy you are!" *Big* can also carry the sense of grown or matured, a sense which overlaps with the idea of size, but not completely. A *large boy* is large in size. A *big boy* is a child that has gotten older and shown some developmental achievement, like eating all of his broccoli.

Even when words overlap considerably, they tend to carve out little areas of meaning for themselves. Or rather, the words themselves don't do this; the people who use them do. Meaning is not something contained in a word but a habit of usage that emerges over time by consensus. A big toe, a big deal, a big spender, a big mistake, think big—you can substitute *large* in these phrases and still be understood, but you'd be working outside the habit, not participating in the consensus. The same can be said about ordering a big Coke or a big pizza.

So how does that habit or consensus come to be? Slowly, over time, from generation to generation; and even after things have changed, very old habits still can show their influence in subtle ways.

Both *big* and *large* are relative newcomers to the English language, meaning they don't show up in written texts until the thirteenth century. Before that, in the oldest English, the word for considerable size was *great* or *mickle*. *Mickle* became what we know today as *much*, and *great* continued along referring to size. The idea of largeness is still cemented in terms like *great apes*, *great blue heron*, *great white shark*, *the Great Plains*, *the Great Lakes*, and *Great Britain* (originally meaning the largest of the British Isles).

But *great* drifted in meaning along a common pathway that assumes what's big is powerful, important, and excellent. These days, in a neutral context like "It is great," the primary sense of *great* is excellent, but the older meanings are still accessible to us. Depending on how formal you take the speaker to be, *great waves* can be excellent waves of the perfect shape for surfing or giant, scary, massive swells.

Big and *large* wander similar meaning pathways, but their starting points were different. The origin of *big* is uncertain, possibly Scandinavian, but in its earliest uses it had to do with strength, vigor, and power. To be *full bigge* in battle was to be forceful and courageous. *Large*, which came in with the French, began with the sense of expansiveness, generosity, and freedom, as in *largesse* or *at large*. Size naturally connects all of these ideas. A bigger hammer falls with more force. A generous donation is a large one. If you have freedom, the space which you can move in is large and wide.

Great, *big*, and *large* shift around, trade places, and overlap in many ways. The places where they diverge hark back to the habits they established early. *Big* still carries the echo of the notion of strength, vigor, and power. For a child to be a *big boy* or *big girl* means that they've acquired not only size but also maturity, a type of power and strength. *Big* has the feeling of vigor and intensity in phrases having to do with emotions like *big fit*, *big argument*, *big love affair*. A *large love affair* just doesn't pack the same emotional punch.

Power and vigor connect to importance, where *big* also claims meaning territory that *large* avoids, such as in *big boss*, *big holiday*, and *big mistake*. Importance connects to popularity, as in "I'm big in Japan."

Big has wider scope than *large*, and there aren't many areas where *large* gets to stake out its own space. Where it does, it carries the echo of the old notion of generous lavishness (*living large*) or freedom from limits (*at large*). This is part of how it managed to claim the area of consumer goods like pizzas, T-shirts, and drinks.

SMALL   MEDIUM   BIG

Through the connection with size but also lavish abundance, things in pieces that could be purchased and consumed for a price attached to *large* in the eighteenth century, such as in *large salt*, *large bread, large coal.* In the nineteenth century, as advertising and marketing kicked into high gear with the number of goods available from the industrial revolution, *large* became the preferred way to name the biggest size of a product. Manufacturers of clothing, bottles of face creams, and boxes of cough drops sold their goods in *small, medium,* and *large.*

We still have those habits when it comes to products. *Small/ medium/large* is repeated and reinforced in this domain constantly. But that doesn't mean new habits can't be established. There is nothing stopping *big* from becoming the term we use for the largest size drink except that there aren't enough people using it this way. If a business wants to distinguish itself by substituting *tall, grande, venti* for *small, medium, large,* it can do just that. The challenge is to get people in the habit of using those terms.

Starbucks managed to get people using their terms by saturating the coffee shop market and being immensely popular, but also because when it began its rise in popularity, it had customers already using slightly unfamiliar terms like *macchiato* and *latte.* A few more unfamiliar terms for sizes weren't too hard to introduce in that situation. And *small/medium/large* still worked. Old habits influence the new habits, giving words like *big* and *large* different domains, but they can also coexist with them.

Crazy English
Why Do We Drive on a Parkway and Park on a Driveway?

This question is a classic staple of the "English is crazy!" routine that has made its way from newspaper humor columns, to letters to the editor, to comedy club stages, to forwarded emails, to internet lists and comment boards. It has been in circulation at least since the 1970s.

It's not really a question that anyone genuinely wants to know the answer to. It's a rhetorical question, looking only for a laugh. It is usually grouped together with similar questions that play up the ways in which English words can take on such varied meanings that they end up sounding like their own opposites. A widely circulated essay, "English Is a Crazy Language," presents a whole collection of these:

> Sometimes I think all the English speakers should be committed to an asylum for the verbally insane. In what language do people recite at a play and play at a recital? Ship by truck and send cargo by ship? Park on driveways and drive on parkways?

There is a lot of fun to be had with the way that English can use the same exact form for nouns and verbs. The verb *to play* sounds the same and is spelled the same as the noun *play*. The verb *to ship* sounds the same and is spelled the same as the noun *ship*. The verb *to park* has the same form as the noun *park*. But this causes only part of the problem with the *driveway/parkway* example. Even though no one is really looking for the answer to this rhetorical question, the way this apparent contradiction came to be can tell us something interesting about the zigzag journeys words can take.

There are many kinds of *ways* in English. Some of them were formed with verbs, like *runway*, *spillway*, and *walkway*. Some of them were formed with nouns, like *railway*, *roadway*, *alleyway*, *archway*, *doorway*, *gateway*, *airway*, *tollway*, *motorway*, *hallway*, and *pathway*. Some were formed with adjectives, like *highway*, *Milky Way*, *expressway*, and *freeway*. Some have even been formed from prepositions like *byway* and *throughway*. *Way* is a very flexible word-joiner.

Driveway was formed with the verb *to drive* in the late 1800s. This was before the automobile, and *drive* was something you did with a carriage or team of animals. A driveway might also be called a *carriageway*, *horseway*, or *cartway*. At the time, no one would have thought of its primary purpose as a place to park anything. Its purpose was to provide room for vehicles to move, not stand still. That's what a barn or carriage house was for. It wasn't until later, with the development of private home driveways leading from the street to a house or garage and the spread of automobiles, that it became standard to park in a driveway.

As it so happens, *parkway* was also formed in the late 1800s, not from the verb *to park* but from the noun *park*. A *parkway* was a broad road for private carriages only, no commercial vehicles, and planted on both sides with trees, grass, and other landscaping. You could always drive on a parkway. The idea for this new type of urban boulevard was first proposed by Frederick Law Olmsted, America's most famous designer of city parks. A parkway was a road for driving through that had the feel of a park.

At the time *park* had already also been a verb for a long time. Since the fourteenth century, a park was an enclosed area of land, and if you fenced in animals or soldiers or equipment on an area of land, you *parked* them, essentially, put them in a park.

Later, the noun *park* took on a more specific sense of an area for ornamental gardens and outdoor recreation, extended from its "fenced-in outdoor area" sense, and the verb *park* took on the more specific sense of "stationing a vehicle in a place" (you could first *park* a wagon or a train) extended from its "putting needed stuff in a designated area" sense. The noun and the verb went their separate ways, the original connection between them becoming a dusty old story for the etymology books.

Now you can park your car on asphalt lots, ferries, and the tenth floor of office building garages, places that are nothing like parks at all. You can also park your car, of course, on a driveway, especially the one in front of your suburban garage. Just as the verb *to park* is stuck in our language habits long after it stopped having anything to do with parks, *driveway* is just a name for a thing in our landscape that used to have something to do with driving but now probably sees more basketball playing. The world and the way we live in it are always changing. It's hard enough to keep up. If we constantly had to come up with totally new words for it too, *that* would be crazy.

What the Hell Is with
What the Hell?

English can be weird, illogical, and annoying. There are many possible ways in English to react to this. "Ugh, English!" conveys disgust. "Oh, English!" is more of a lament. "Really, English?" conveys impatient incredulity. But "What the hell, English?" just gets the whole complicated feeling with all its emotional layers. Frustration, dismay, indignation, and aggravation plus a tinge of put-upon disappointment.

Fitting, then, that the phrase *what the hell* is itself one of those weird things about English. It just doesn't add up. It doesn't get its meaning from its pieces. Granted, that is often the case with idiomatic expressions. We don't get the meaning of "raining really hard" from the *cats* and *dogs* in *raining cats and dogs*. The meanings of the words *piece of cake* don't add up to the meaning "easy." Phrases often get their meanings as wholes. There's nothing unusual about that.

But even in those cases, the words in the idiom tend to at least be valid as combinations, the types of words that can go together. *Raining cats and dogs* has the same types of words as *dropping pens and pencils*. *Piece of cake* is like *slice of pizza*. *What the hell* doesn't have that. *What* can start a wide array of exclamations (What nonsense! What a day! What big teeth you have!), but you do not usually find *what* followed by the definite article *the* (What the nonsense? What the day?) except in *what the hell*.

OK, make that except in *what the hell* and all of its related phrases with substitutions for *hell*: *heck, hey, devil, deuce, dickens*, and a range of, let's say ... stronger words. *What the X* is productive as a phrase type, but substituting the word *hell* with alternatives doesn't change the meaning at all—an annoyed, exasperated meaning. It can only make it a little more or less intense.

The hell has served as a little enhancement you can stick in to express exasperation at least since 1785, when "How the hell came you here?" appears in court testimony. Before that, in the sixteenth and seventeenth centuries, a similar use of *the devil* is common in phrases like *what the devil is this?* Before that all the way back in the fourteenth century *devil* shows up in this use, but without the *the*, in phrases like "What devil have I with the knyf to do?" from a line by Chaucer, meaning "What the hell do I have to do with the knife?"

This early use was probably influenced by the French phrase *que diable*, "what devil," which can still be used as a translation for *what the hell?*, though it's apparently a little more old-fashioned sounding in French.

The path to the "the hell" intensifiers seems to have gone from *devil* to *the devil* to *the hell*. There were detours along the way as nicer substitutes for *devil* were devised like *dickens* and *deuce*, and sometimes phrases with the indefinite article *a* were used, such as in "What a pox is the matter now?" Later, blander, less tied to eternal damnation versions like *what on earth* and *what in the world* became popular.

Even though we can trace the path that led to *what the hell*, we still can't really explain why the *the* got in there in the first place. But it's a crucial part of the construction now, so much so that even a simple "What the?" is enough to show how much we're shaking our heads and throwing our hands up.

Like most of the parts of English that don't seem to make sense, it got to be that way for some reasons we can explain and understand. But also some we can't. English is like that sometimes.

What the hell, English?

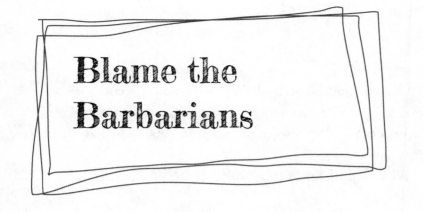

Blame the
Barbarians

Language changes, and change introduces lumps and bumps and flaws in the system, but a lot of what makes English weird has to do with what didn't change, what got held over from the earliest layers of the language. For those oddities we can blame the barbarians.

Who were the barbarians? *Barbarian* is the historical name for the uncivilized other. The ancient Greeks came up with it and used it to refer to the peoples of the non-Greek world. To them, Greek was the language of civilization, and other forms of speech were just meaningless babble. *Blah blah blah* said these strange others, or rather *bar bar bar*, which is how they came to be called *barbaros*.

The Romans adopted the term and used it for the tribes they encountered who were not Roman or Greek. As they expanded their empire, they came in contact with all sorts of barbarians. Many of the tribes they interacted with in Europe (through subjugation, alliance, or fighting) spoke Germanic languages.

The story of how English got to be the weird way it is begins with those Germanic languages and the barbarians who spoke them. During the fifth century, an assortment of them poured across the North Sea, from what is today Denmark, the Netherlands, and northern Germany, and conquered most of England. These tribes—Jutes, Saxons, and Angles—planted themselves on the island. A millennium and a half later, we speak the descendant of the languages they brought with them.

There were already people on the island when the Germanic tribes got there. These people spoke Celtic languages. Latin was also used, since Rome had ruled England for hundreds of years, but mostly in official, administrative domains and not among the general population. After the Romans left in 410 AD, the barbarians began their conquest.

And it was much more of a conquest than the Roman one had been. Rome ruled from afar, with the necessary apparatus to claim territory and resources and hold off invaders, but the Celts they ruled over went on living their lives with their own culture and language. The barbarians, in contrast, came in droves and came to vanquish.

The Celts were killed or driven out or absorbed into the new way of life. Very little Celtic influence remains in English, and what little there is is mostly in place names. English is at its core a Germanic language, and its story begins with those invading hordes.

After about a century of the Germanic tribes taking over and settling in, the Romans returned. This time it was not soldiers but missionaries who arrived, and they came not to conquer but to convert.

The monks who came to convert the island to Christianity brought their Latin language with them, and they also brought the Latin alphabet. Their mission depended on words, on texts: scriptures, parables, homilies, prayers. They set about translating these texts into the language of the people they encountered, a language that by this time had coalesced into something that, although not totally unified (there were regional differences and dialects), was English. Specifically, what we now call Old English.

There were sounds in this barbarian language that Latin did not have and had no way to represent in the Latin alphabet. The monks tried out their own solutions to this problem in different ways in different monasteries that left us with some strange spelling quirks. But for the most part, the writing of Old English was pretty regular, based on the principle that things should be written as they sound.

That changed as the language changed and as more layers of influence were laid down over and over again. There will be more blame to assign. But first there is also another group of barbarians to blame, different Germanic-speaking barbarians who added their own layer of weirdness.

About two hundred years after the monks arrived and started Old English on its way to a written, literary language, the Viking invasions began, and they kept up for a few hundred years. These Vikings spoke a different language from the Anglo-Saxons, but a related one—Old Norse, the language that eventually turned into modern Swedish, Danish, Norwegian, and Icelandic.

The Viking invasions began as smash-and-grab raids to take as much as possible and go, but some groups decided to settle down and make a new life on the land they claimed. Their language was similar enough to Old English that they could communicate with the Anglo-Saxons without too much difficulty, and over time their own way of speaking mixed into the surrounding language, leaving vocabulary and expressions behind that don't quite fit the rest of the pattern at the old Germanic layer.

Much of the Scandinavian influence in English is so well absorbed that it doesn't cause any weirdness. For example, there was a sequence in Germanic that became a 'sk' sound in Scandinavian and a 'sh' sound in English. When we mixed some Scandinavian words into English, we got some doubles like *skirt* and *shirt*, but we don't even think of those as the same word, so the intrusion is unnoticeable.

There are a few noticeable bits, however, that we can blame specifically on the Viking barbarians, such as our two different ways of saying the 'g' sound (see "Getting and Giving the General Gist") and what the *egg* is up to in the expression "egg someone on" (see "Egging Them On").

The rest of the issues in this section put the blame on the barbarians in general, which is to say, they come from the Germanic habits laid down early in the language. Some of the exotic (from the Roman point of view) sounds they used created a spelling mess that is still with us today ("Thoroughly Tough, Right?"). We also see their lingering influence in the words we use, such as irregular verbs (see "I Eated All the Cookies"), and in words we could use but don't (see "It Goes By So Fastly"; "Elegantly Clad and Stylishly Shod"; and "Six of One, Half a Twoteen of the Other"). They also left some effects on phrasing, such as why the expression is "Woe is me" and not "Woe am I" (see "Woe Is We").

English has changed so much in the last thousand years that almost nothing in Old English looks familiar if you haven't studied it. Being a speaker of modern English barely helps you at all. But while most things have changed, some things have held on, like stubborn barbarians, claiming territory and kicking up trouble.

Thoroughly Tough, Right?

Why Don't *Tough, Through,* and *Dough* Rhyme?

When you see a *gh* in an English word, how should you pronounce it?

It stands for an 'eff' sound in *tough* and *laugh*. Also *cough*, and *enough*. But wait, it also stands for nothing in *though*, *dough*, *daughter*, and *caught*. And then you've got *night*, *light*, and *right*, *eight* and *neighbor*, *thought* and *sought*, and, well, you get the idea. There are all these ways to say it, or not say it, but in none of them does it actually stand for the sounds *g* and *h* are supposed to represent: 'guh' and 'huh.'

There is a reason for this mess, and it begins about a millennium and a half ago when a group of Roman missionaries landed on English shores with their Latin texts in their Latin alphabet.

The Latin alphabet was pretty well suited to the Latin language, but not so well to the strange Anglo-Saxon language they found on this rainy island. It had exotic sounds that Latin didn't have, and when scribes had to sit down and work out a way to translate texts into the local language, they had to figure how to write these sounds. They could maybe stick in some runes, those scratchy-looking native symbols that the locals used for some of the sounds. Or they could try to find the closest match in the Latin alphabet. But then they had to decide which one was the closest match. There were various ways to go with this.

They tried a whole bunch of approaches, and for a few hundred years they switched it up a lot. There was no standardized spelling for a long time. Eventually, for one of those exotic sounds, we settled on *gh*.

OK, so which sound was it? Well, another problem here is we don't even use that sound in English any more, except in a few cases, like for that sound of disgust, that back-of-the-throat rough vibration found at the end of the word *blechhhh*.

Linguists call it a velar fricative. You'll also find it in *yech*, *ichh*, and *ughh*, but you can hear it in a few more wordy kinds of words too—the composer *Bach*, words from Yiddish like *tuchus* or *chutzpah* or from Scottish like *loch* or the name *Lachlan*. We can say it when we need to, but over the centuries we just kind of kicked it out of English.

German still uses it, though, and a look at some words in German will be helpful in our quest to figure out what's going on with the English *gh*. What's "to laugh" in German? *Lachen*. There's a velar fricative in the German word (spelled with a *ch*) and a *gh* in the English counterpart.

Let's take a look at some other pairs:

daughter	*Tochter*
eight	*acht*
light	*Licht*
night	*Nacht*
right	*recht*
high	*hoch*
thought	*gedacht*
neighbor	*Nachbar*

Lift an English *gh*, and you're likely to find a German velar fricative underneath. That's the sound the *gh* used to stand for.

This is a little misleading. It makes it seem like English came from German and changed some sounds along the way. English doesn't come directly from German; rather, both German and English, and a number of other languages as well, come from an earlier, more ancient language, and that language had a *blech* sound of some kind. Depending on the language that ancient language developed into—Dutch, Swedish, Danish, German, Scottish, English, and so on—that *blech* sound might still be a *blech* sound, or a softer, gargle sound, or a 'sh' or 'k' or 'g' or 'h' sound, or it may just have disappeared altogether.

Lucky for us, even though it disappeared, we still get to see where it used to be. The *gh* is like a fossil imprint left by the long-ago speakers of our language. A little reminder that these same words were said by other mouths, centuries away, in their own, different way.

That's pretty cool. But kids who are trying to learn how to spell or English learners trying to figure out how to pronounce things probably aren't too won over by this "Hey look at the cool fossil!" take. It's frankly a little unfair that we somehow got stuck with this spelling system that creates a whole extra hurdle for people. The other languages that came down from that ancient ancestor of English don't have it so bad. They didn't end up with all these silent letters, even though some of the sounds they used to have did go away.

Making it even more complicated is the fact that in some cases, the *blech* sound didn't go silent in English but turned into an 'f' sound. This happened inconsistently, over hundreds of years, while the spelling system was not yet standardized and pronunciation varied from one part of the country to the next.

In some places people said *tough* with the *blech* sound and in other places they said 'tuff.' Some said *through* with the *blech* sound and some said 'thurf' or 'thruf.' Some said *dough* with the *blech* sound and some said 'duff.' In cases where the *blech* sound was kept, it often weakened into a vowel and disappeared. Today, the pronunciation of *tough* has settled into the 'f' version, and *through* has settled into the vowel version. *Dough* has also settled into the vowel version, but *duff* lives on in the name of traditional English desserts like *plum duff*.

The vowel sounds in *tough*, *through*, and *dough* (approximately 'uh,' 'oo,' and 'oh') also went through many changes over the years. They differed from each other from the beginning, as *toh*, *purh*, and *dah* in Old English (where *þ* stands for a 'th' sound and *h* stands for the *blech* sound), and they were accordingly spelled with different vowels. Then the French brought in their way of spelling words with *ou*. At first it was used to represent an 'oo' vowel (as in French *vous*), but that habit was adopted haphazardly, and in the midst of other sound changes that were in progress (see "Peek, Peak, Piece, People").

When the dust cleared and the spellings were firmly established by habit, *ou* had the vowel sound of *tough* in words like *country*, *trouble*, and *young*; the sound of *through* in words like *routine*, *group*, and *you*; and the sound of *dough* in *poultry*, *shoulder*, and *soul*. But most of the time it had the 'ow' vowel sound of *house*, *cloud*, and *plough*.

Even if you were somehow aware of the places where the *blech* sound used to be, it wouldn't help you predict a number of other places where *gh* can show up. Some spellings come straight from the spelling conventions of other languages, like the *gh* in *spaghetti* or *ghost* (see "Uninvited Ghuests").

And once the *blech* sound disappeared, *gh* took on a life of its own and got extended to other words. *Furlough*, for example, never had the *blech* sound at all. It was borrowed from the Dutch *verlof*, and was at first spelled *furlof* or *forloof*. Perhaps on analogy with *cough*, people started writing *furlough*. Perhaps on analogy with *thorough*, people started saying *furlow* (that spelling also occurred into the nineteenth century). The sequence of letters *ough* no longer had independently working parts within it. It stood, as a whole chunk, for 'off' or 'ow' or 'oo' or whatever other sound it could be matched to in an existing word.

This happened for other *gh* chunks too, like *igh*, *eigh*, and *augh*. *Delight* and *sprightly*, originally *delite* and *spritely*, were modified under the influence of *light* and *right*. *Sleigh*, borrowed from the Dutch *slee*, was made to look like *weigh*, perhaps to avoid looking like *slay*. *Haughty* was modeled on *aught*, because, well, *hawty* just doesn't look very *haughty*. The 'gh' may no longer stand for a particular sound of its own, but it still makes a difference in the overall look and feel of a word.

The Latin alphabet was never meant to cover all the possibilities for all the sounds in the many languages of the world. But people have figured out ways to adapt it to their needs. Sometimes it involves accent marks, other characters, or capital letters, and sticking two letters together to stand for one sound has been a pretty useful adaptation. Or it can be if the language doesn't stop using that sound. If it does, things can get thoroughly tough.

Getting and Giving the General Gist

Why Are There Two Ways to Say the Letter *G*?

The graphics interchange format, GIF for short, made it possible for us to enter a new era of easily shared cute animal pictures and animated reaction shots, but it also brought trouble and strife to the English-speaking world in the form of a linguistic disagreement. How do you say *gif*? With the hard 'g' of *give* or the soft 'g' of *ginger*?

The *g* has been trouble for a long time in written English. Early on, the 'g' sound was written with a letter developed by Irish scribes, an open-looking *g* with a flat top known as the insular *g*. It looked like this: ȝ, and it stood for a few different sounds: a hard 'g,' a soft 'g,' a 'y' sound, and a sort of soft gargle we no longer use in English.

Before consonants or the back vowels 'a,' 'o,' and 'u,' it had a hard 'g' sound. Before the front vowels 'i' and 'e,' it was soft. This is also the case in French (*garçon* vs. *gentil*) and is still basically the case in English (*game, go, gum* vs. *gin, gel*).

It wasn't necessary to have different letters to stand for the different sounds, because the sound was predictable from the sounds next to it. But as the Vikings continued to raid, invade, and settle in England from the ninth century on, they complicated the *g* situation. Their language, Old Norse, was pretty similar to Old English and had come from the same Germanic ancestor, but they hadn't softened the 'g' before front vowels the way English had.

For example, the word for yellow had been something like *gelwaz* in that ancestor. In Old English, the 'g' before 'e' softened into the 'y' of *yellow*, while in other Germanic offspring, it stayed a hard 'g' (Danish/Norwegian/Swedish *gul*, German *gelb*).

A similar thing happened with the verb *to give*. In the proto-Germanic ancestor it was something like *geban*, and this became 'yive' in English and *gefa/give/giva* in the Scandinavian languages.

Then the Viking version of *give* began to catch on. Regions where people once said 'yive' started saying 'give.' Other 'g'-before-a-front-vowel words spread too, like *get* and *gear*. Once enough people were using these hard 'g' pronunciations, it started to turn into a spelling issue. If you had a written word like ʒear or ʒet, it was no longer clear from the surrounding letters whether that ʒ stood for the 'g' sound in *gear* or the 'y' sound in *year*, the 'g' of *get* or the 'y' of *yet*.

At the same time, the French had taken over and a new layer of vocabulary was being laid down. There was a new letter in town too, the round-topped *g* from the continent. Scribes started to split up the functions: the old ʒ style for the 'y' and other soft 'g'-type sounds as in ʒear (*year*) and the continental *g* for the hard 'g' of *gear*. Then, that old style ʒ took on a new shape as a letter called the yogh, which looks like a quick and loose version of the old ʒ: ȝ. It's all over the place in manuscripts from the 1200s and 1300s.

But the yogh didn't last. The French scribes didn't like to use any of those strange English characters adapted to strange English sounds. They did bring in the *j*, though, which gave us a way to write the soft 'g' in loans like *justice*, *jar*, *journey*, *join*, and many, many others. And they preferred using the more familiar *y* for the initial sound in native English words like *year* and *yet*.

Eventually English writing settled into a sloppier version of the French approach to g words, with *g* representing a soft 'g' before front vowels and a hard 'g' before consonants and back vowels . . . except in some words like *give* and *get*.

Those just happen to be some influential words! Even though there are far more g words that follow the soft 'g' before a front vowel rule, the ones with the hard 'g' are extremely common in everyday language and have lots of possible forms to show up in (*giving, gift, given, get on, get down* . . .). They are constantly out there, shoring up their own sound pattern, making it hard to decide how to say infrequent words like *giblets* or new words like *gif.*

We owe it to the Vikings, who had no idea the yift they were yiving us.

Egging Them On

What Is the *Egg* Doing in *Egg On*?

When someone eggs you on, they are trying to provoke and encourage, but with a bit of a naughty glint in their eye. They're probably trying to get you to do something stupid.

Where does the egg come in to all this? Are you being compelled to act under the fear of having eggs thrown at you? Do you expect to have egg on your face after you've done the foolish thing you're being spurred to do?

It turns out there was never an egg involved at all.

The *egg* of *egg on* goes back to the same ancient Germanic root (historical linguists hypothesize *agja*) that turned into *edge*. It had senses related to the edge, or sharp side (or point), of a sword. Good for poking someone along to compel them to do something. Or goading them by sharpening it. In Old English that root turned into something pronounced with a softer 'g' sound than it became in Old Norse, the language of the Vikings. One of the things that differentiated Old English from Scandinavian languages was the softening, or palatalization, of 'k' and 'g' sounds in certain contexts.

Where Norwegian has *brygga* (pier), we have *bridge*. Where Swedish has *slägga*, we have *sledge* (hammer). Where Danish has *ryg*, we have *ridge*.

After the Viking invasions of England in the 800s, Old Norse–speaking Danes settled down in eastern areas of the island, and over the centuries the cultures and languages intermingled. English speakers borrowed the Old Norse expression meaning "to incite or provoke," to *edge on*, except the Old Norse pronunciation of *edge* was 'egg,' and this was borrowed too.

At that time, the English word for egg the food was pronounced similarly to German *ei*, so there need not have been any confusing *egg* with *edge on*. However, in the dialect of the north, where there was more influence from Old Norse, people started saying *egg* with a hard 'g' at the end, the Scandinavian way. (In Old Norse the ancient Germanic roots for *edge* and *egg*, *agja* and *ajjaz*, had become homophones, as 'egg.') In other words, English borrowed the verb *egg*, meaning "incite," from the Scandinavians. Then it also borrowed the pronunciation of the noun *egg*, meaning "the thing chickens lay," from them as well.

But not all at once. William Caxton, who introduced the printing press in England, was also a publisher and translator of ancient works into the English language. In the prologue to his 1490 translation of Virgil's *Aeneid*, he addresses some of the difficulties he faced in trying to decide which English words to use so that the greatest number of people could understand them. As an example, he tells the story of a group of merchants who went in search of food somewhere on the banks of the Thames while waiting for the winds to change so they could sail on. One of them, from the north, "axyd after eggys." The "good wyf" answered that she could speak no French. When the merchant, who also could speak no French, began to get angry, another merchant stepped in to ask for *eyren*, which she readily understood.

For a long time during the Middle English period, part of the country continued to call eggs *eyren*, or *eyer*, or *eyron*. Because the important city of London was in the south, that dialect tended to set the standards for the language, but in the case of eggs, the northerners, more closely bound to the Viking descendants, took the lead and incited a change. You might say they egged it on.

I Eated All the Cookies

Why Do We Have Irregular Verbs?

Kids are so good at learning languages. Even their mistakes are genius.

They say things like, "I Eated all the cookies!" and "I drinked all the milk!" And why shouldn't they? That's how those words should work in a reasonable language. Everyone knows what they are trying to say when they do this, because what they have done is make a logical extension from the information presented to them. *Eat* and *drink* are verbs. Past tense verbs end with *-ed*. Put those facts together. Done.

And we laugh at them for this?

Eventually the cute mistakes stop. Kids grow up and fall into line with the rest of us and learn to stop being so darn logical. They get used to the fact that some verbs don't fit the expected pattern.

If the pattern is so clear a child can see it, why are there verbs that don't fit the pattern? Why do we even have irregular verbs?

Our irregular verbs weren't always that way. In fact, they used to be regular. Which is not to say that the past tense of to *drink* was once *drinked*; rather, the past tense used to be formed by a different rule. The old rule didn't add an ending but made a change to the vowel. In Old English, the past tense of *drincan* was *dranc*. And this was the regular way to do it. Other words like it followed the same pattern:

to sing
singan, sang

to find
findan, fand

to climb
climban, clamb

to cringe
cringan, crang

That particular vowel-change rule was not the only one. Verbs belonged to different classes, each of which had a different rule. You could tell which rule to use based on the form of the root word. Verbs of the *ride* type got the past tense according to the following pattern:

to ride
rīdan, rād

to glide
glīdan, glād

to chide
cīdan, cād

Words of the *stand* type followed yet another pattern:

to stand
standan, stōd

to shave
scafan, scōf

to bake
bacan, bōc

Some of the forms created according to these rules survived into modern English. The past tense of *to drink* is still *drank*. We still have *sing-sang*, *find-found*, and *stand-stood*. But many of these old past tense forms didn't survive, though it would be kind of cool if they had. We'd be able to say "After the coach *chode* the skier for holding back, he *crang*. But the next day he *glode* past the competition, *shove* a minute off his time, and finally *clamb* up to the winner's podium."

So what happened to those forms that didn't make it?

Well, in addition to those vowel-change rules, there was one other past tense rule in Old English. It held for words like *lufian*, "to love," which became *lufode* in the past tense. The verbs that fit into this class in Old English formed the past tense with the addition of a 'd' or 't' sound at the end:

to kiss
cyssan, *cyste*

to deem (judge)
deman, *demde*

to allow
aliefan, *aliefde*

to fill
fyllan, *fylde*

to believe
beliefan, *beliefde*

This class is the origin of the regular past tense suffix we know today, ending with either a 'd' sound as in *loved* or a 't' sound as in *kissed* (it's a 't' sound even though we spell it with a *d*). Starting around the year 1100, this way of forming the past tense spread to words in the other classes, and it eventually forced out the other patterns. This probably had to do with the fact that French words were being borrowed into English, and it was easier to add something to the end of a borrowed word than mess around with the vowels in the middle. *Glode, chode,* and *shove* gave way to *glided, chided,* and *shaved. Clamb* became *climbed. Boke* became *baked.*

But some verbs resisted the spread of this pattern, and they became the irregular verbs we know today. Words like *ate, drank, took, found, knew,* and *spoke* didn't give in to the *lufode* pattern. They stood firm. They became irregular because the world changed around them while they refused to change.

But what was it about the verbs that didn't give in? What gave some verbs the strength to resist the spreading change? If you take a look at the irregular verbs in English, you'll notice that they happen to be some of the ones we use the most. Because we used them so frequently, their forms were reinforced over and over again, bolstering them enough to withstand the changes around them. Less common words didn't get their forms reinforced enough to resist. Sadly, we just weren't saying *glode* and *chode* often enough to keep them alive.

Even today, while some words like *dream* and *kneel* show some wavering between regular and irregular patterns (*dreamed* or *dreamt*? *kneeled* or *knelt*?), the really frequently used ones like *sleep*, *leave*, and *feel* resist full regularization. *Sleeped*? *Leaved*? *Feeled*? No way.

And the really, really frequently used verbs, like *to be*? They tend to be the most irregular of all, and they trace back to even older patterns and ancient historical changes.

Of course, this is a simplified account of a complicated story. Sometimes old past tense forms can survive even if they aren't frequent at all, because they belong to particularly notable domains of use. We don't use the verb *to smite* very often, but when we do, *smote*, with its stern ancient Germanic sound, just seems to fit the scenario better.

And the pressure to change isn't all one way, from irregular to regular. *Had* and *made* were once *haved* and *maked*. Sometimes when a regular verb is very frequently used, it can lose some sounds, making it become irregular. Why keep pronouncing those extra consonants if you don't really need them? *Had* and *made* are good enough.

Likewise, why put that extra syllable in *hitted, cutted,* and *shutted* when they already end in a sound that's close enough to the past tense suffix?

Every act of language use involves a mix of enforcing old habits, applying rules to new situations, and economizing effort. The proportion of the mix is subject to varying priorities and is always changing. It may not make for a very orderly product, but it does the job we need it to do.

It Goes By So Fastly

Why Do We Move Slowly but Not Fastly?
And Step Softly but Not Hardly?

Adjectives say something about the qualities of nouns. A cheetah is fast, a sloth is slow. A pillow is soft, the floor is hard. Adverbs are similar to adjectives, but they say something about the qualities of verbs, or the manner in which something is done. A dependable way to make an adverb in English is to add a *-ly* ending to an adjective. You can walk lazily, speak honestly, complain beautifully, cook loudly—the adverb adds almost any kind of manner to almost any kind of verb, and *-ly* can attach to almost any adjective. One can write Chekhovianly, text LOLingly.

So why does English stop you from moving fastly or stepping hardly?

While most adverbs in English are formed with *-ly*, a few stay bare in this role. Come again *soon*. Lie *low*. Aim *high*. Walk *tall*. These would be strange as *come again soonly, lie lowly, aim highly, walk tally*. On the other hand, it's not very strange at all for adverbs that can take *-ly* to show up as bare. *Drive safe, play fair, buy cheap,* *think different*—these are all normal things to say, even if sticklers might object to them as too casual and suggest you add that *-ly*.

Both bare and *-ly* forms have been around as adverbs since the earliest days of Old English. There was *cwiclice* (quickly) and *oferflowendlice* (superfluously or "overflowingly") alongside *hāte* (hotly) and *cealde* (coldly). That *-e* on the end was pronounced as a second syllable, an 'eh' sound, and it was an adverb ending of its own. There was *wid* (wide) and *wide* (widely). *Georn* (eager) and *georne* (eagerly).

Many of the word endings of Old English were lost over time, including the *-e* adverb ending, leaving *faste* as *fast* and *hearde* as *hard*. The adverbs that had an *-e* ending instead of *-lice* from way back are more tolerated today, even by sticklers, in bare form. Who can argue with classic-sounding phrases like "The wind blew cold" or "The sun shone hot"?

By the 1500s *-ly* had become the preferred way to form adverbs, though bare forms continued to be used and even gained a little ground in the eighteenth century. But something happened in the nineteenth century that made the -*ly* forms truly, wholly, and fully take over. What happened was grammar books.

In the booming industry of language advice books, bare adverbs, otherwise known as "adjectives used as adverbs," were discouraged. No matter that "indifferent honest" had come from Shakespeare; it should be "indifferently honest." People became insecure about their adverbs and started to add -*ly* just to be sure.

Still, there were a few words that -*ly* just wouldn't stick to, even if it had attached at one time or another. *Fastly* had been used a few times, to mean *quickly*, including by Shakespeare. And *hardly*, in the sense of strongly or with force (as opposed to softly), was common for a while. One could "step hardly" or "strike hardly" or "bite hardly." In Shelley's *Frankenstein*, Dr. Frankenstein, after bringing his creation to life, spends a sleepless night during which "sometimes my pulse beat so quickly and hardly that I felt the palpitation of every artery."

But this sense of *hardly* fell out of use as another one took its place, the sense we use now meaning scarcely or to a small degree in phrases like "I hardly slept" or "you can hardly tell." That sense grew out of the use of *hardly* to mean "with difficulty," as in "I could sleep, but it was hard." We don't use it that way anymore though. "He's hardly changed" does not mean he changed with difficulty but that he's barely changed at all.

Fastly, though never much in use, also had a different sense. We mostly use *fast* to mean speedy or quick, but that came out of an earlier meaning of being firmly fixed or stable, as we have preserved in phrases like *stand fast* or *hold fast*. It picked up its connection with speed through its connection with vigor (to hold fast is to hold strongly) and with closeness, as in *fast beside me*. You could at times cleave fastly, believe fastly, and even walk fastly. But it didn't necessarily mean you did it with speed.

So *fast* was the much more common form of the adverb from the very beginning, with its origin in the Old English *faste*, and the *-ly* form was tried here and there but didn't catch on. *Hardly* was claimed by another meaning space, blocking its use in other places. So we are left with an asymmetry in the adverb pairs *slowly/fast* and *softly/hard*.

But the asymmetry is not the fault of the bare forms alone. We can flip it around and say that maybe *slowly* and *softly* don't need their *-ly* all that much. After all, when we run slow or fall soft, it doesn't sound too casual or incorrect. The *-ly* adjective has certainly become the most productive and standard way of making an adverb, but not because it's the one true correct way. As a well-respected guide to English by fancy Harvard scholars put it in 1901, when the rule against using bare adverbs was in full force, these adverbs are "an ancient and dignified part of our language, and the pedantry which discountenances them is not to be encouraged." Not very plain put, but clear said.

Elegantly Clad and Stylishly Shod

Why Is It *Clean-Shaven* and Not *Clean-Shaved*?

Coffee is fresh-brewed, olive oil is cold-pressed, fruit snacks are freeze-dried, hillsides are sun-drenched, and dapper swells are sharp-dressed. A very common and productive way of forming an adjective in English is to join a word—adjective, adverb, or noun—to a past participle.

The past participle is the form of the verb you use in the perfect tense. *I have brewed. You have pressed. He has dressed.* The participle is usually formed by adding *-ed* to the root verb, but many frequently used verbs in English have an irregular form of the past participle. It isn't *I have knowed* but *I have known.* Not *you have writed* but *you have written.* Adjectives formed using those irregular verbs use the irregular past participle. So celebrities are *well known*, books are *ghost-written*, shy people are *soft-spoken*, and championships are *hard won*.

Clean-shaven is an odd case because the past participle of *shave* is not *shaven* but *shaved*: *I have shaved, you have shaved, they have shaved.* Shouldn't we say *clean-shaved*?

Shaven, like *known*, *written*, *spoken*, and *won*, is a remnant of the Germanic verb inflection system of Old English. When we keep an old form like that despite all the centuries of intervening change that left most verbs with an *-ed* ending instead, it's usually because the verb is so frequently used that the old form has simply become fortified habit, so it stays. In the case of the verb *shave*, the habit wasn't so well fortified that it kept *shaven* from giving way to *shaved*, but *shaven* has managed to hang on longer as an adjective, especially in the specific form *clean-shaven*.

There are a number of adjectives that preserve the old form, even when the verb it comes from has moved on with the times. *Sodden*, the adjective for thoroughly soaked, was originally the past participle of the verb *seethe*, meaning "to boil." You could peel the shell off an "egge wel sodden" or feast on sodden meat. These days we still use the verb *seethe* in the metaphorical sense of boiling with anger, but the past participle is regular *seethed*. "Each time his team has lost the playoffs, he has sodden with anger" is a strange thing to say, indeed.

It's a similar situation for the regular verbs *melted*, *loaded*, and *shaped*, which have echoes of what they used to be preserved in the adjectives *molten*, *laden*, and *misshapen*. Even irregular verbs like *drunk* and *sunk* show their old, even more Germanic habits in the adjectives *sunken* and *drunken*.

Why wouldn't adjectives go ahead and change with their corresponding verbs? Once a word has spun off into another part of speech or expression, it can go its own way. If there's a context where a specific word gets repeated enough to become a habit, it doesn't really matter how it's treated in other contexts.

So *cloven* survives in the context of the *cloven hoof*, *smitten* lives on in *smitten with*, and *trodden* keeps its old form in *downtrodden* and *well trodden*, even as the verbs *cleave*, *smite*, and *tread* become ever less frequent.

The *graven* of *graven* images doesn't even have a corresponding verb anymore. It was originally from the Germanic root that became *graben* in German and *grafan* in Old English and meant dig or engrave. In the sixteenth century, English, under the influence of French, which had itself borrowed the Germanic root and formed *engraver* out of it, started using *engrave* as the verb and jettisoned the original—except in the case of *graven images*, where the old past participle lives on as an adjective in one, very specific, biblical context. *Engraved images* sounds like perfectly normal English, but it doesn't sound like something you'd call false idols.

Once a specific context for an irregular form is well established, it can sound awkward to use its more regular, familiar counterpart. Although it's possible to be *shaved, sheared, clothed,* and *shoed,* it sounds much less awkward (though a bit fancier) to be *clean-shaven, neatly shorn, elegantly clad,* and *stylishly shod.*

We know that language has its odd twists and turns and places where it doesn't seem to make sense. But numbers—when you want some clarity, some logic, some consistency—numbers are where it's at, right? And English number words are organized into a pretty consistent system. For example, if you see three digits in a row, you can look at it and instantly know how to say it, even if you've never seen it before:

One in the hundreds position, so *one hundred*.
Six in the tens position, so *sixty*.
Eight in the units position, so *eight*.
One hundred sixty-eight.

Again, the system is so reliable that you can use it to pronounce number words you've never heard or said before. Have you ever heard anyone say *four thousand nine hundred and eighty-two* before? The chances of you having heard any one particular number in the thousands are small, but it doesn't matter. You know, from putting it together with the system, both how to say it and what it means.

Other words don't work the same way. Have you ever heard the word *capriole*? Unless you're into dressage horses, probably not, and you're not going to figure it out just by piecing the parts of the word out. (It's a horse leap with a back kickout of the legs, by the way, but you can't know that from just looking at the word.) Number words have a predictable system that other words don't.

But in a few places the predictable system falls down. *Eleven? Twelve?* Shouldn't that be *one-teen, two-teen*? It could have been so perfect. We could have had it so good. What are you doing, English? Why'd you have to go and mess it up?

Etymologists can trace the words *eleven* and *twelve* all the way back to a time even before Old English, to some proto-Germanic stage, when *eleven* was something like *ainlif*, or "one" *lif*, and *twelve* was something like *twalif*, or "two" *lif*. All the Germanic languages were left with remnants of this stage (e.g., German *elf, zwölf*, Dutch *elf, twaalf*, Swedish *elva, tolv*). What did this *-lif* mean? One guess is that it is from a root for "to leave." *Ainlif* is "one left," as in one left after counting to ten, and *twalif* is "two left" (after counting to ten). Or it might simply be an ancient version of a word meaning "ten."

So then the question might be: Why don't we have *threelif, fourlif, fiflif, sixlif,* and so on? Well, a long, long time ago, when the number words were first being formed, most people didn't have much reason to distinguish numbers above ten. They didn't have bank accounts, or keep track of calories, or memorize dates for history class. So the basic number words up to ten formed first, and then they were extended a bit with the -*lif* ending.

There may have been at one time a further elaboration along this line, a *threelif, fourlif*–type system, but even in that case, *ainlif* and *twalif* would have been used more often than the other *lifs.* That's because the numbers eleven and twelve are simply more useful. Many number systems are based on twelve. It's divisible by the most numbers. You can share twelve things with three, four, or six people. That's hard to do with ten. You can also count to twelve on one hand. You use your thumb to count off three knuckles on each of the other fingers. Even though we use a number system based on ten, we've got twelve inches to a foot, twelve hours on the clock, and even a special word *dozen* because twelve is just so useful.

EGGS!
CHEAPER BY THE
TWALIF

So if some long-ago terms for eleven and twelve were being used more frequently, their forms would have stuck, even when another system started to develop.

Not that the rest of the teens are all neat and logical. In the rest of the system we say the tens place first—*FORTY-four*, *NINETY-two*. But the teens are different. We don't say *TEN seven*, but *seven-TEEN*. The tens place comes second. Plus it's not *ten* but *teen*.

Until we get past fifty, we have all kinds of irregularities of pronunciation. *Twenty*, not *twoty*. *Thirty*, not *threety*. *Fifty*, not *fivety*. Those forms also got stuck through habit. We've been making everyday use of those numbers for longer than we have for two hundred, three hundred, four hundred, and so on.

Other languages have other departures from neat order. Latin eighteen and nineteen were "two from twenty" and "one from twenty." Spanish has special words up to fifteen and switches at sixteen. Italian and French switch at seventeen. The French word for eighty comes from the idea of "four twenties." Danish fifty is from "half third times twenty." At different times, in different societies, certain numbers took on their names through habit, probably because those numbers were socially significant and got more practical use.

The words we needed earliest and used the most frequently are usually the most irregular. *Eleven* and *twelve* were about as high as we needed to go at some point. Their weirdness is a sign of their importance.

Woe Is We

Why Is It *Woe Is Me,* Not *I Am Woe?*

Woe is slightly old-fashioned as a word but can act pretty normally in sentences. It's a fusty sounding replacement for *sorrow, misery,* or *emotional distress.* You might see it in phrases like *river of woe, full of woe, woe to my enemies, time of woe, economic woes, heartfelt woe,* or *tale of woe.* But you're most likely to see it in *woe is me,* the deliciously dramatic way to register a complaint with the universe.

This phrase is not acting normally. If it were, the expression would have a more familiar structure, like "Woe am I," or even better "I am woe." Why, in this specific phrase, does regular grammar seem not to apply?

"Woe is me" was first formed long before Shakespeare had Ophelia say it in act 3 of *Hamlet.* It dates back to Old English, when English grammar worked differently and shared more in common with its Germanic relatives.

Back then, English had something called a dative case. The dative case is used for an indirect object or where we would now have a preposition. For example, "This is difficult for me" was *Uneaðe me is ðis* ("Difficult me is this"). "Here is my child who is very dear to me" was *Her is min cild þe me is swiðe leof* ("Here is my child who me is very dear"). The preposition *for* or *to* isn't necessary in those examples because the dative form of *me* includes that sense. This sense hangs on in phrases like "She gave me a dollar," where the meaning is "She gave a dollar to me." The phrase "Woe is me" did not mean "Me and woe are one and the same thing," but rather "Woe is to me" or "Woe is unto me." The dative sense is clearer in biblical phrases like "Woe unto them."

All of the words in *woe is me* go back to the oldest, Germanic layer of English. *Woe* is a close relative of Gothic *wai*, Old Saxon *wē*, Swedish *ve*, and German *weh*. The verb *is* also has many Germanic relatives. In Old English, *me* once varied in form depending on whether it was the direct object of the sentence (*mec*) or the indirect dative (*me*). Now the distinction has been lost, but it carries on in German, which has *mich* and *mir* for "me," depending on its role in a sentence. The German version of the expression is *Weh ist mir*

(Woe is [indirect object] me), not *Weh ist mich* (Woe is [direct object] me) or *Weh bin ich* (Woe am I).

Yiddish, another language that has held on to a distinction in the me-pronoun with *mikh* and *mir*, has the well-known expression *oy vey!* which can be translated as "Oh, woe!" and is a shortening of the phrase *oy vey iz mir* (oh woe is [indirect object me), not *oy vey iz mikh* (oh woe is [direct object] me) or *vey bin ikh* (woe am I).

The dative is also in play for another archaic term that seems grammatically odd to our modern ears: *methinks*. The *thinks* in *methinks* is not from the verb *think* we are all familiar with but from a different Old English verb meaning "to seem." *Methinks* means "it seems to me." *Me* has the dative sense "to me" in that phrase.

Woe is me is another one of the many phrases in English that are handed down whole to us from history with bits of old Germanic grammar locked in place. We just have to put up with it. Woe is we.

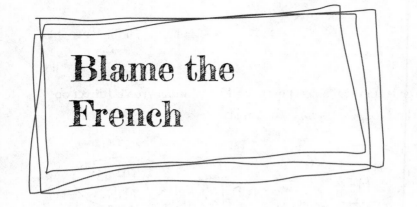

Blame the French

By the turn of the first millennium the Germanic-speaking *folk* of England had a settled civilization and a language of their own that could now be called *Englisc*. It had an established written tradition and a literature. Of course, it was subject to all the normal forces that make languages shift and mutate: dialect differences, sound changes, generational drift. It was also transformed by incursions from groups speaking other languages, especially the Vikings.

But it was pretty stabilized, and if it had stayed on the path it was on, we would be speaking a very different English today, probably something more like Dutch or one of the dialects of northern Germany. Old English would have continued to change, as all languages do, and turned into a modern version of itself, as did Dutch, German, and all the descendants of the Germanic barbarian languages. Instead it became something weirder. For this, we can blame the French.

In 1066 William the Conqueror, the Duke of Normandy, came over from France to defeat the English king and claim the throne. Anglo-Saxon leaders, landholders, and church officials were replaced by the conquering Normans. For the next few hundred years, England was controlled by French speakers. But the majority of people in England, those who did not rule, preach, study, or own land, did not become French speakers. They kept on speaking English. The ruling language did manage to mix its way in, however, and not just with a few words here and there. The French infusion changed English in profound ways.

Ironically, the Normans themselves had once spoken a Germanic barbarian language, Old Norse. A little more than a century before conquering England, the Normans were "Norse men," Vikings who had settled in northern France. But they had quickly adapted to French ways, including feudalism and Christianity, and abandoned their language. There are very few remnants of that language in French. Just a few nautical terms and the word *havre*, meaning haven or harbor, which is the name of the largest port city in Normandy, Le Havre.

In contrast, the French that the Normans adopted and brought to England is everywhere in English. Because they controlled all official institutions, the vocabulary of government and land administration came to be overwhelmingly rooted in Norman influence, with words like *govern, rule, advise, fines, tax, balance, debt, account,*

money, measure, estate, rent, tenant, and *pay.* Also the language of law, in *court, contract, crime, heir, judge, sue, claim, appeal,* and *proof.* More general terms having to do with the organization of society like *city, village, mayor, servant, stranger, custom,* and *marriage* also come from this early wave of French, as do *battle, challenge, power, conquer, courage, cowardice, duty, honor,* and *dignity.*

French also burrowed deeper into layers of the language that were not just about the structure of social institutions. Generally speaking, the words with the most fundamental connection to our prehistoric human essence come from the oldest Germanic layer of the language. *Love, hate, eat, drink, heart, lungs, earth, water,* and *sun* all go back to Old English and before. But a certain elemental level of ourselves and our surroundings also came to be represented by French imports such as *comfort, cruelty, cry, grieve, dance, feast, delight, joy, pain, envy, fruit, flower, farm, garden, mountain, river,* and even *air.*

After the conquest, English and French were divided by social class. The ruling elite spoke French and the lower classes spoke English. Eventually, French influence spread to English, but English remained a Germanic language in its basic structure and grammar and much of its most basic vocabulary. French was layered into it, mostly in vocabulary, but in a few other subtle ways. It wasn't because the ruling class imposed the French language on the lower classes and forced them to speak it. It was because over time the ruling elite adopted English as their own language.

Naturally, because the ruling elite were still educated in French, they often reached for terms from French when speaking English. And as written English, which had all but disappeared for a while, returned in literature, education, court records, and town ordinances, people had to figure out how to use English in these formal domains. They also had to make decisions about how to spell words that had gone on developing and fracturing into dialects in spoken form for years without the moderating direction of a written standard. French habits were already there, ready to be of service. And they were, to such an extent that English became the most Frenchified Germanic language it could be.

Latin was also a big influence in English from this point on in a couple of different ways. Some Latin was introduced through French, since it was itself a language descended from Latin. But since Latin was also used in education, the church, and scholarly work, words were also borrowed directly from Latin. In many cases it is unclear whether an English word came in from French or from Latin. Hundreds of words that have a Latinate prefix (*pre-*, *de-*, *sub-*, *in-*, etc.) were imported into English by people familiar with both French and Latin. An educated person using English could form *prepare* from *préparer* or *praeparāre*, *decide* from *decider* or *dēcīdere*.

So we can blame the French for transforming the vocabulary of English, not just by introducing French words in almost every aspect of life but also by providing an easy gateway to Latin borrowing and word creation. This torrent of words didn't force English words out but wove its way through different channels of society, creating multiple vocabulary types where versions of the "same" word (in English, French, or Latin) took on subtle (or not so subtle) differences in connotation and meaning.

Louis Hjelmslev, a twentieth-century Danish linguist, said English, "this so-called easy language," was "more difficult than anything else that I have tried to learn." Even though his native language was Danish, a pretty close Germanic relative of English, and he was fluent in French, he thought that "what makes English difficult is the choice of words, the choice of the right word and the proper wording in the right place." He actually did speak English too, but he considered it deceptive, seemingly easy at the beginner stage but becoming "bottomless and endlessly complicated" in what it demanded the more one learned.

The vocabulary explosion is not the only thing we can blame the French for (see "A Sizeable, Substantial, Extensive Vocabulary"). It introduced new word stress patterns that created confusion and splits based on stress alone (see "Don't InSULT Me with That INsult!"). It left behind old word forms and phrase ordering (see "Without Fail," "Ask the Poets Laureate"). It even encouraged the development of a new English speech sound with its own letter, v (see "Of Unrequited Lof").

The conquerors brought their language but eventually gave it up. In doing so they left a bottomless and endlessly complicated mark on English.

A Sizeable, Substantial, Extensive Vocabulary

Why Are There So Many Synonyms?

The English lexicon: it's big. Also large, sizeable, substantial, huge, enormous, hefty, immense, extensive, and voluminous. English is not unique in having synonyms—most languages do—but it is notable in being rife, teeming, overrun, and crawling with them.

We can blame the French for this one, or at least for getting it all started. When the Normans took over, they brought their language, but they didn't use it everywhere. French was the language of ruling elites and their institutions of administration, government, and law. The elites also used Latin for education and in the church. Often it can be hard to tell whether a word in English came through French or through French speakers using Latin.

The common people continued speaking English, and that linguistic split between the classes survives in some of the synonyms we have today where the word from the Germanic base is earthier and less refined. Words of the *folk* versus words of the *people*. The best-known example of this split is in our animal names. In the fields and farms, where the Anglo-Saxon peasants worked, they get their old Germanic names. On the tables where the Anglo-Norman nobles dined, they get their Romance names.

calf	veal
cow	beef
pig	pork
deer	venison

There are plenty of other areas where the word that came from French carries a bit more status:

leader	captain
teacher	professor
house	mansion

or high-class sheen:

dirt	soil
stool	chair
craft	art
meet	encounter
love	adore
want	desire
wild	savage

In the centuries following the French rule of England, the English language spread back into all areas of life, common and official, in a new mixed form with a vocabulary full of words that had come from French but were completely Anglicized. Words like *farm*, *city*, *village*, *fruit*, and *flower* now belonged to both the nobility and the folk. But the language continued to expand under the influence of French and Latin as literacy and education spread and people adopted new words to indicate a similar elevated status or prestige. Educated doublets were adopted for more formal or academic contexts:

hate	detest
bug	insect
warning	alert
understand	comprehend
brotherly	fraternal
behead	decapitate
to be	to exist

This kind of thing happened in all the languages of Europe after the Renaissance, but English had had a long head start and had already absorbed so much so completely that there were plenty of cases that left no trace of prestige difference at all. Is one of these pair members fancier or more elite than the other? Certainly none of these pairs are as clearly different as *bug* and *insect*.

woods	forest
odd	strange
uphold	support
mark	sign
shape	form
shut	close
fair	just
kind	sort
bliss	joy
freedom	liberty

Many of the French words that were adopted displaced older English words (e.g., *beauty* replaced *wlite*, *clear* replaced *sweotol*), but the old words sometimes carved out specialized corners of their own where they could survive (see "Couth, Kempt, and Ruthful"; "Elegantly Clad and Stylishly Shod"). *Ruth* was replaced by *pity*, but *ruthless* managed to continue to live alongside *pitiless*. *Seethe* was replaced by *boil*, but in figurative uses, like *seething with anger*, it hung on. *Worldly* was not replaced by *mundane*, but the senses separated. Both words started out meaning "of the world" (as opposed to "of heaven"), and now they mean nearly the opposite of each other, "sophisticated" versus "boring." English absorbed a lot while keeping a lot, and that made the vocabulary grow . . . and increase.

The effect on the vocabulary went further than just the words themselves. English also acquired parts to build with. Fragments to attach to other words. Suffixes that took on a life of their own once they had entered on the coattails of enough words.

Endings like *-ation*, *-ance*, *-ify*, *-ment*, and *-able* were not part of English until they came in with French words. But after there were enough of them to make a noticeable pattern, they became their own, active part of English that could be used to make new words within the language. Words like *purify*, *ignorance*, *temptation*, *accomplishment*, and *changeable* came in with French words that were rooted in Latin, but their endings became independent enough for English speakers to attach them to Germanic roots in words like *speechify*, *utterance*, *starvation*, *fulfillment*, *breakable*, and many others.

So many others. This development led to the creation of even more synonyms. You could have *improvement* and *betterment*, *legible* and *readable*, *ridiculous* and *laughable*. Words can be borrowed and also created in-house. This is true of other languages too, but English has for centuries had two deep wells to draw from.

Don't InSULT Me with That INsult!

Are There Noun-Verb Pairs That Only Differ by Stress?

There are a number of noun-verb pairs in English that are spelled exactly the same and pronounced exactly the same, except that a different syllable gets the stress depending on whether it's a noun or a verb. In these cases, the verb has stress on the second syllable (we conDUCT an interview, reCORD a history, inSULT an adversary), while the noun has stress on the first syllable (the good CONduct, the extensive REcord, the shocking INsult).

English at its historical core, the old Germanic one, is a language that always puts stress on the first syllable in a two-syllable noun. The oldest English words, the elemental ones, the ones that have been part of the language since before the Romance language–speaking continentals arrived on English shores, follow this pattern: *mother, father, water, meadow, iron, apple, liver, marrow.* It is still the case that a high percentage of English words have first-syllable stress.

The pattern was a little bit different for verbs. Verbs could have prefixes, like *be-* and *ge-* and *for-*, that didn't take the main stress, so you could have verbs with second-syllable stress like *beGIN, forGET, unDO.* But most verbs were what are now single-syllable words (*eat, drink, love, help, give, take*) that usually appeared with verb endings, so they had the pattern of two-syllable words with stress on the first one (*GIVeth, HELPest, TAken*). First-syllable stress was the overwhelming general pattern for verbs, with a little flexibility added in from the prefixed ones.

Then came the French vocabulary onslaught. The earliest borrowings were quickly assimilated to the English way. French final-syllable stress became English first-syllable stress: *monTAGNE-MOUNtain, jarDIN-GARden, forÊT-FORest, citÉ-CIty, monNAIE-MONey, jourNÉE-JOURney.* But later borrowings often didn't adjust (*maCHINE, diVORCE, balLOON*). They kept their French ways but still became fully English words. (French stress rules are more complicated than "final-syllable stress," but to the English ear words appear final stressed.)

Between those two points came a large number of words from French or Latin (or both) that had noun and verb forms. French *demand/ demander* gave us *a demand* and *to demand.* Latin *respectus/ respectare* gave us *respect* and *to respect.* Today, many of them have stress on the second syllable for both noun and verb (*reSULT, surPRISE, aLARM, desPAIR*). But there are also a large number that have stress on the first syllable for both (*PROmise, PROfit,*

COMfort, CONtact, PREview). There are also some that have the noun-verb difference in stress like *INsult/inSULT*.

However, none of these noun-verb pairs have first-syllable stress on the verb and second-syllable stress on the noun. If there is a split, the noun has first-syllable stress and the verb has second-syllable.

When these words came in with the stress on the second syllable, sometimes both noun and verb settled in and remained that way, with perhaps a slightly foreign air about them. Sometimes both got pulled, from the overwhelming peer pressure of English first-syllable-stress words, toward their own first-syllable rhythms. Sometimes only the noun was pulled. There was an enormous mass of nouns already in the language promoting first-syllable stress. The verbs were under less pressure to shift because they had the company of a small group of second-syllable stress words with prefixes (like *beCOME*) to make keeping that stress pattern easier to accept as English.

The French and Latin borrowings in the group were not elemental, everyday concepts like *water*. They moved in scholarly, educated, cultured domains, places where people spoke French and studied Latin, where they were fully aware of the prefix status of Latin prefixes in Latin words (*con-, re-, sur-, pro-*, etc.) and so were able to comfortably treat them in a similar way to English prefixed verbs like *become*. The vast majority of verbs with Latin prefixes still have second-syllable stress.

But the pull of the first-syllable pattern is strong. And plenty of verbs waver between second- and first-syllable stress. What about *research*? ("Did you REsearch the question? Did you resEARCH the question?") *Transform*? ("Did it TRANSform your under-standing? Did it transFORM your understanding?") And there are plenty of paired nouns that seem to be in the midst of this wavering too (*my REsearch/resEARCH, my ADdress, my adDRESS*). Even some of the late borrowings that are clearly French (*homage, mus-tache, perfume*) can go either way. In many later borrowings, the British and American stress preferences differ.

Switching between these stressed pronunciations can elicit a strange confusion about which one feels right, to the point where you start to doubt your own judgment. In a sense, the language as it is wants to have it both ways. Two habits, one descended from the oldest layers and one added in with the French/Latin influx, compete with each other. As I was putting examples together, I ran into this confusion over and over again. It usually went something like this:

Protest is a syllable-switching N-V pair. The noun is PROtest and the verb is proTEST ... or is it? "He came here to pro-TEST against the new policy" "He came here to PROtest against the new policy." Wait, the first-syllable version sounds better. Doesn't it? But in "The lady doth proTEST too much" it's gotta be second syllable. Or in the phrase "I proTEST." Huh. But you can also say "I PROtest." But that means some-thing a little different. The first is an objection. The second means I go to a demonstration of some kind. Right? Oh, English ...

This uncertainty about *protest* points to yet another area of compli-cation. A verb can have second-syllable stress (I *proTEST!*), become a noun with first-syllable stress (I am organizing a *PROtest*), and then become another verb based on that noun (Did you *PROtest* last weekend?), recycling back into the vocabulary as a verb with a slightly different meaning.

Verbs like *to access, to contact, to pressure, to compost*, and many, many others never even started with second-syllable stress be-cause they were formed off of nouns that already had first-syllable stress.

You may be ready to throw up your hands and give up ever trying to predict anything about how to stress English verbs, but if you take a historical view, you can get pretty far. When it comes to verbs, if it has two syllables and it looks Latin-y with obvious Latin-y prefixes, the stress is probably on the second syllable (*pro-VIDE, subSCRIBE*), but not if it looks like the verb came from the noun (*to COMpost, to PREview*). What's more, even if it looks Old English-y and has an English-y prefix, the stress is probably on the second syllable (*beFALL, withDRAW*). Otherwise, go first syllable (FOL*low*, WHIS*per*).

When it comes to nouns, if it has two syllables, the stress is probably on the first one. If it's clearly from French, it might be stressed differently (*baguette, ennui*), but it has long been the case that as words lose their obvious connection to French, they can shift their stress. This can lead to dialect differences where British and American speakers differ on where they put the stress in *ballet* or *debris*, or where some American speakers say *POlice* or *JUly*, or "*CEEment.*" It causes a whole lot of trouble for *pecan*, which we got from an Algonquian root through French explorers who said *paCAHN* and English speakers can't quite decide how to pronounce.

So who is to blame for this mess of stress? Some of it lies with the French, who brought in a new stress pattern with a whole bunch of Latin-derived words. Some of it lies with our old "barbarian" impulse to keep the stress up front (except on prefixed verbs). Some of it lies with the snobs, who liked to show off their familiarity with

French sources and Latin word structure and who brought in even more educated Latin words as modern English was taking shape. Words like *obturb* (to disturb), *subsalt* (to jump), and *exquire* (to seek out) were tried (see "Blame the Snobs").

The words that didn't make the cut during this period look funny to us now, but the ones that did are completely normal, if maybe sometimes slightly educated-sounding. We trade a bit of confusion about word stress for the way they enrich our vocabulary.

Without Fail

Why Is It *Without Fail* and Not *Failure* or *Failing*?

Without fail is such a common, normal thing to say that it's hard to see anything weird about it, but it's actually pretty different from other *without* phrases. *Without* is a preposition that takes a noun or noun phrase. *Without cheese, without a bun, without the grilled onions.*

So what is the *fail* in *without fail*? Is it a noun? If so, it sure is a strange one. Can you have a lot of fail? Can you announce a fail? Sure, there is a recent development in language play where people make internet video compilations of the "best fails" and memes about "so much fail!" but *without fail* has been around for centuries and has none of the cheeky sense of wordplay about it that the modern *fail* noun has.

When *without* wants to go with verb-y concepts, it goes with verbs that have been converted into nouns by various means. One way is to make a gerund with *-ing*, so that the verb *cook*, for example, becomes the noun *cooking*, as in *cooking is fun*, or *I went three days without cooking*.

Another way to make a verb into a noun is through various word endings that convert them. Just as you can do something without *organizing* or *deliberating*, you can do it without *organization* or *deliberation*, without *resentment* or *attachment*, without *approval*, s*urvival*, *arrival*, *disposal*, without *erasure*, *closure* . . . there are so many ways to get to the noun you need. *To depart* has *departure*. *To fail* has *failure*.

Of course, there are some nouns, and some pretty important ones at that, that look just like their corresponding verbs: *Love*, *hate*, *trust*, *fear*, *regret*, *sleep*, *change*. All can act as verbs or nouns, and in their role as nouns, all can appear after *without*. *Fail* is not one of these nouns.

> *Love is blind.*
> *Change is gonna come.*
> *Fail is not an option?*

Of the words that most commonly follow *without*, most are noun gerunds: Things go without *saying*. People do things without looking, knowing, thinking, or realizing. There are also many frequent *without* expressions that use nouns derived from corresponding verb forms: *without hesitation, permission, complaint, interference, justification*.

Why is *fail* such an under-the-radar outsider? *Fail* came to English in the early days of the French infusion. The verb *faillir* meant to be wanting, to lack, and it was used in English with that meaning, such as in the phrase "five failen of fifty" to mean five less than fifty. It also had the senses of losing power, proving deficient, being unsuccessful in an attempt, and a whole constellation of senses related to lack and falling short that it still has in our verb *to fail*.

The noun *failure* came much later, in the seventeenth century. It was formed in English from the verb *faillir*, but the end syllable was confused with a different suffix, *-ure* in words like *figure, pressure*, and *closure*. Due to this confusion, *faillir* became *failure*. But before that the gerund form *failing* was used as the noun, in *failing of teeth, failing of eyes, failing of the spirit*, and also *without (any) failing*. For a while, there was also another noun form, *faille*, taken directly from French.

Sans *faille* meant without fault, lack, or flaw, and it worked its way into medieval English along with other common set phrases like *sans doute, sans délai, crier merci, en bref, au large, par cœur*. We made the words more English but kept the basic structure: *without a doubt, without delay, cry mercy, in brief, at large, by heart*.

Without fail proved useful, and over time its meaning changed from without fault to predictably, reliably, without exception, as in "Every morning he gets there ten minutes early, without fail." Meanwhile, in modern French, *faille* came to mean a flaw or break, most specifically a geological fault line. And failure, as in the opposite of success, was taken over by a completely different word, *échec*.

Fail and *fault*, in both English and French, have a long history of converging, diverging, swapping, and expanding meanings, but *sans faille* got Anglicized to *without fail* and stayed that way.

A standard rule of English is that the adjective goes before the noun. You can have a tasty lunch followed by a good nap, but not a lunch tasty followed by a nap good.

There was some flexibility in the order of noun and adjective in Old English because there were more word endings that told you what role a word had in a sentence. So word order could be freer. But the order adjective-noun has been the way it's done for centuries. In Shakespeare there is some word ordering that looks strange to us now (What light through yonder window breaks?), but the adjective-noun order is prevalent and robust throughout the tales of *violent delights and violent ends*, *empty vessels*, *guilty minds*, *false hearts*, and *strange bedfellows*.

So how do we get a phrase like *sum total*, a phrase so common that it doesn't seem strange at all—that is, until you take a closer look and wonder why it's not *total sum* instead.

Total sum is a thing that's possible to say in English, but it doesn't exactly mean the same thing. A sum is a quantity. Add a bunch of quantities together and you've got a whole quantity of quantities. A total sum. If I tell you that the price is the cost of the product, plus tax, plus shipping, you can ask: What is the total sum? What's the cost when you add those sums together into one total?

But when you say "That's the sum total of my knowledge" or "My job performance is not the sum total of who I am," you mean something a little more abstract, something that doesn't necessarily involve sums at all. The *sum total* is the total extent or the essence of something.

It is possible for *sum total* to mean the same thing as *total sum* in cases like "You will be reimbursed for the sum total of travel expenses." That is how the phrase got its start in the fifteenth century, in simple cases where numbers or costs were added together. The reason the adjective followed the noun was because of French.

In French the normal ordering is for the adjective to follow the noun, as can be seen in French phrases that we borrowed as is: *femme fatale, film noir, carte blanche, cause célèbre.* When the French-speaking Normans conquered England, French became the language of official institutions and practices. That happens to be the area where we find a large number of noun-adjective phrases today. Terms like *attorney general, heir apparent, body politic, notary public, court martial, fee simple,* and *ambassador plenipotentiary* all belong to the domain of officialdom. As does *time immemorial,* which originally referred to time "out of memory," or before recorded time, a concept that mattered in considering whether certain customs had the force of law.

Other official domains like the academy (*professor emeritus, poet laureate*) and the church (*friar minor, mother superior*) also carried over titles in the French way of doing things. Latin was also used in these domains, and the adjective ordering was reinforced by the similar Latin way of doing things, where phrases like *diabolus incarnatus* gave rise to *devil incarnate.*

Often it's difficult to say whether French or Latin is the source. There was both Latin *summa totalis* and French *somme totale* to support the creation of *sum total.* Whatever its ultimate source (and it's probably both, considering the way French and Latin coexisted in institutions of authority), it did become a fully English expression.

Did the French takeover of official life cause English to acquire a new grammatical rule, ordering adjectives after the noun?

Not exactly. Mostly it acquired a number of set phrases, learned as wholes, not created by productive rule. But because there were enough terms to create a type of pattern in specific domains, the pattern could be extended. The existence of *lieutenant general, deputy general,* and *vicar general* makes the later *postmaster general* and *surgeon general* not only possible but, as positions of official responsibility, expected.

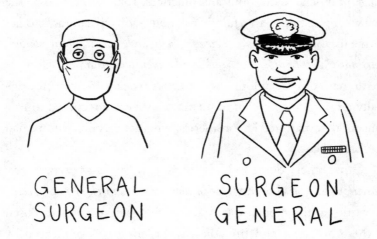

GENERAL
SURGEON

SURGEON
GENERAL

Even after French was replaced by English in official operations of the country, noun-adjective phrases continued to exert some influence. Intellectual discussions of *matière philosophique* or *matière esthetique* kept their basic form (and more of their high intellectual flavor) in English discussions of *matters philosophical* and *matters aesthetic.* It has that same fancy sheen when extended to jokey phrases that never occurred in French at all, as in "I'm an expert in matters mixological."

Maybe a "lunch tasty" and a "nap good" don't work, but speaking of a "banquet paradisiacal followed by a somnolence luxurious" sounds much more allowable. Extremely pretentious, but English nonetheless.

Of Unrequited Lof

Why Isn't *Of* Spelled with a *V*?

The little word *of* is one of the most frequently used words in English and does all kinds of work. It can relate to spatial position (north of, to the left of), not having something (cured of, deprived of), or having something (full of, loads of). It can show origins, motivations, and causes (of hearty English stock, of his own volition, what did they die of?) as well as what things are made of (bed of roses, suit of armor) or what the topic is (dreams of, thoughts of, tales of, songs of). It denotes general ideas like possession (a necklace of mine, that car of yours) and specific, harder-to-define ideas like being a particular example of a class of items (the month of May, the city of Oslo). The only way to properly define *of* is with a long, long list of all the ways it can be used. In fact, it's such an integral part of the fabric of our language that we hardly notice in this little word of just an *o* and an *f*, there's no 'f' sound at all.

The *o* is not an 'o' sound either, but we're used to vowels shifting around in fuzzy ways. There's also no 'o' sound in *love* or *above*. Those words are just weird in a regular way. But if they were spelled *lof* or *abof*? That would be truly weird. No other words but *of* end in an *f* pronounced as a *v*.

Of can be traced back to the earliest days of written Old English in the exact same form it has now. *Of* has changed by adding new constellations of meanings and uses, but it hasn't changed its spelling. Does that mean that because there is no 'f' sound in *of* now, it must have changed its pronunciation?

No, not really. *Of* has been pronounced 'uv' since Old English. What changed was that those speakers couldn't hear that 'v.' They said it, but they thought they were saying 'f.'

What does this mean, and how could I possibly know the internal thought processes of people who lived a thousand years ago? We only have to look at our own thoughts about the 'l' sound today. There are two different versions of this sound, depending on where the *l* occurs in a word. At the beginning of a word like *leaf* we use a "light l" made with the tip of the tongue. But at the end of a syllable, like in *feel*, it's a "dark l"—more of the body of the tongue is raised, and it sounds less clear, darker. This is a change so subtle you normally can't even hear or feel the difference. But you CAN hear it when someone fails to make the change. It gives them an accent.

For example, one aspect of an Italian accent comes from the fact that the Italian language only uses the light 'l' and not the dark 'l.' So "I feel good" becomes "I feelll good." Che bello!

This will also mean that an American or British speaker might have an accent when speaking Italian. They'll use the dark 'l' when they shouldn't and instead of *dolci* with a light Italian 'l' say something like "*doalchee*."

For the English speaker, light 'l' and dark 'l' are the same sound. The difference between them is completely conditioned by their placement in a word. We wouldn't think to try to spell them differently. For Albanian speakers, however, they are different sounds. There are words in which a light 'l' or dark 'l' in the same position causes a word to have a different meaning. Light 'l' *lum* is river, but dark 'l' *llum* is sludge.

A thousand years ago, English had an 'f' sound that in some situations was pronounced like what we would call a 'v' but that speakers would not even notice was different from any other 'f.' If an 'f' came before an unstressed vowel, as in *wulfas*, the plural of *wulf*, the 'f' was produced with vibration of the vocal cords, the sound we know as 'v.' Even though we no longer form the plural with -*as*, we see that old pattern reflected in pairs like *wolf-wolves* (also *elf-elves, self-selves, knife-knives, loaf-loaves*, etc.). This process was also conditioned by the situation where the 'f' was followed by the endings which formed verbs, reflected today in pairs like *thief-thieving*.

Of and *off* were the same word in Old English, both spelled *of* but pronounced differently. 'Off' was the pronunciation with word stress, and 'uv' was the unstressed version. They did not fully become separate words until the seventeenth century.

But well before that, English developed a new speech sound, the 'v.' People were already producing it (like the dark 'l' now), but under the influence of French it became a separate speech sound.

First, because of the habits and perceptions of French scribes, it began to be written differently.

Whereas before the French took over in 1066, English would borrow Latin *v* words and make them fit English (*verse* in Old English was borrowed as *fers*), after the conquest, French *v* words like *vain*, *valour*, *veil*, *vine*, and many others made their way into English texts with their *v*'s intact. After a while, the letter then made its way into native English words that used the 'v' sound. In written texts, *wolfs* became *wolves*, *loafs* became *loaves*. Eventually, the difference between the 'f' and 'v' sounds began to matter to the language to the point where we now have plenty of pairs of words where it makes the only difference: *van/fan, vine/ fine, invest/infest*.

So why did *of* never become *ov*? Because *of* and *off* were not seen as different words until long after the *v* change took over. Like *of*, the words *is* and *was* had different pronunciations based on whether they were unstressed ('iz,' 'wuz') or stressed ('iss,' 'wass'), but eventually the unstressed version with the 'z' sound became the thing to say in all situations. We never changed those spellings to reflect the pronunciation either. But also, the stressed versions pronounced 'iss' and 'wass' never took on their own meanings like *off* did.

Suppose they had. Suppose 'iz' was the pronunciation for most uses of the word *is*, but another use arose from a stressed position, like the end of a sentence. Suppose *iss* came to mean something more specific, like "existed for an impressively long time." We might say "Mount Rushmore is old but the Grand Canyon iss."

This is an awkward hypothetical, but it captures the somewhat messy, complicated persistence of *of* and *off*. Two words, two pronunciations, and a shared, entwined history that iss.

Blame the
Printing Press

A few centuries after the Norman conquest, by the end of the 1300s, English was again a written language. Though French and Latin were still considered the proper, formal means of written communication, spoken English had worked its way back up through the nobility to the highest levels. Even the king spoke English.

English returned not only for practical purposes like record keeping and public proceedings but for literature as well. Aristocratic patronage supported the production of written manuscripts of English poetry. Chaucer, who moved in courtly circles for most of his life, had established a new foundation for the art of written English by the time he died in 1400.

But there wasn't yet a standard for how English should be written. There were not enough examples to follow at this point. The language had changed too much to just revive the Old English tradition, and because the language hadn't been subjected to the standardizing forces of official usage, there were extreme dialect differences between regions. There was no agreement on the correct way to write or spell to use as a guide. It was up to each author or scribe.

Some standards started to emerge after the Court of Chancery, the court that handled contracts, trusts, and land disputes, switched to English in about 1430. A large number of official government documents were created in London over the next few decades. This loose, emerging standard came to be known as Chancery English, and though it doesn't use all of our modern spelling conventions, it's readable to us today. Still, it wasn't codified, just a collection of individual choices by individual scribes that often differed a lot. If it could be understood, it was good enough. There were a lot of documents to produce, and the handwriting labor was intense.

Then, in 1476, a merchant named William Caxton brought an amazing new invention back to England from the continent: the printing press. Now texts could be made much more quickly and get around much more widely. And those texts would take their spellings with them. In a bit of outstandingly unlucky timing, this happened to take place during the middle of a major shift in English pronunciation. When it was over, homophones, homographs, and silent letters littered the landscape.

Caxton was a merchant, a member of a growing class that was able to acquire a certain amount of education and literacy. He was working in Flanders when he started a printing press in Bruges. Printing had been spreading through Europe for a few decades, but most of the works produced were in Latin. The first work that

Caxton printed was in English: his own translation from French of a retelling of the legend of Troy. He had written a manuscript translation that had become so popular among the English-speaking courtiers of the Burgundian Netherlands (the duchess was the sister of the king of England) that he couldn't keep up with demand.

Producing manuscripts took too long. He invested in a printing press and printed his popular English translation. After honing his craft for a few years, he returned to England and set up a press near Westminster Abbey, where he started cranking out English books. He also printed some works in Latin and French, but he had a merchant's eye for what would sell, and vernacular was where it was at.

There were no style guides or copy editors, and faster production was better business. The spelling of a word in any particular place might depend on how it looked in the original manuscript, the choices of a translator, or the habits of a typesetter. An extra letter might be added to make a line come out looking more even.

A few might be taken away to secure the straightness of a margin. People didn't fret about spelling inconsistencies (though they would much later). The books were readable.

Printing gave more people more access to the printed word than they ever had before. More education was possible. Literacy increased. With more people becoming accustomed to reading in English, expectations developed about how English should look. This is still true. Our own expectations are built around what we already do. Yer ekspektayshunz meyk yoo krindge if ai rait laik this beecuz uv hau yoo lernd too reed and wut yer yoozd too seeying.

Despite the inconsistency, certain habits and expectations were established as printing spread. Those habits reflected how the language was spoken at the time, at least in some specific dialects. But over the same years the spoken language was changing. From the fourteenth century to the seventeenth century, the vowel system of English underwent a massive reorganization called the Great Vowel Shift.

To give just one example, the words *food*, *good*, and *blood* all once had the same vowel sound, a long 'o' as in *boat* (*boat* itself was once pronounced more like *bought*). There were many other changes and they happened at different paces in different places. Some dialects still haven't made all the shifts.

The Great Vowel Shift was a complicated and drawn-out process, and some of the shifts were undone by subsequent changes in certain words. It significantly affected the spelling system, because while people began by writing words according to how they pronounced them, when later generations said them differently, they sometimes changed the spelling to fit their pronunciation and sometimes stuck with what they were already used to. Also, sometimes the newer pronunciations were considered vulgar (these kids and their "good food!" I eat "goad foad"!), so even when everyone was saying it the new way, the writing habits, always more formal and conservative, stayed the way they were. To this day, even within the standard language, some words like *roof* still waver between pronunciations. But the spelling is not going to change.

By the time the Great Vowel Shift had spread through most of the country in spoken language, the writing system, aided by the printing press, had solidified into a standard that was taught, propagated, and reinforced constantly. It was full of spellings that represented pronunciations that were sometimes hundreds of years out of date.

Old vowels were not the only thing the printing press helped fossilize. It also preserved old consonants from Old English that were no longer pronounced and French and Latin spellings of words inserted into texts by people who were used to writing in French and Latin.

The pieces in this section cover situations where it was the printing itself that directly created spelling issues, as when the typesetters Caxton used introduced their own spellings for words ("Uninvited Ghuests"). There are also examples of indirect effects, where a profusion of printed works so well established the look of certain words with silent consonants, apart from how they were pronounced, that the spelling spread to other words so they would fit in with that look, rather than for any sound consideration ("Gnat, Knot, Comb, Wrist"; "Coulda, Shoulda, Woulda").

I also cover questions of vowels and how the way they are written departs from the way they are said ("Peek, Peak, Piece, People"; "Crew, Grew, Stew, New . . . Sew?"). The printing press didn't make our letters, decide how they should represent sounds, or create a spelling system. But it took decisions made loosely and on the fly, spread them around, and turned them into stronger habits.

Uninvited Ghuests

Why Are *Ghost, Ghastly,* and *Ghoul* Spelled with *Gh*?

The *gh* pair of letters is all over the vocabulary of English, from *aught* to *wrought*, and it can stand for a variety of different sounds, as it does in *night*, *laugh*, and *through*, but it rarely starts a word or stands for the hard 'g' sound, as it does in *ghost*.

Usually, when a *gh* stands for a hard 'g' sound, it's because we borrowed it, like we did with *ghetto* and *spaghetti* from Italian and *ghee* and *dinghy* from Hindi. But *ghost* was not borrowed; it goes back to the Germanic ancestor language, like *go* and *goat* do. It's about as old an English word as you can get. Somehow it ended up haunted with an *h*.

Ghost had no *h* until the 1500s. At first it was spelled *gást*, and other words having to do with fright were formed from it, including *gastliche* and *agast*. Those too became haunted by the *h*, giving us *ghastly* and *aghast*. What changed in the 1500s was the spread of printing.

William Caxton, the man credited with introducing the printing press to England, got his start in the printing business in Flemish-speaking Bruges, where he set up his first press. After a few years, he returned to London and established an operation there.

Typesetting was a new, time-consuming, and difficult task, and it was convenient for Caxton to set up shop with people who already had experience with it, even if they weren't as familiar with English spelling conventions, which were still not standardized anyway. Flemish (the variant of Dutch spoken in Belgium) came from the same West Germanic family that gave rise to English and had many similar words with slightly different pronunciations. The usual Flemish spelling for a hard 'g' sound before a front vowel like 'ee' was *gh*. The word for ghost was *gheest*. When these typesetters came across words that reminded them of their related Flemish equivalents, they were naturally inclined to use spellings closer to what they were used to.

In the early works printed by Caxton the word shows up a lot in the phrase *holy ghost*, and over time the printers' habit became everyone's habit.

Before the printing press, a convention from French had been established where the soft 'g' sound of *July* was spelled with *j* before the back vowels 'a,' 'o,' or 'u' (*journey*) and a 'g' before the front vowels 'e' and 'i' (*general*). But sometimes there was a hard 'g' sound before a front vowel, and for some of these situations writers used the French method of *gu* to represent that sound (*guess*, *guide*). The Flemish-influenced typesetters instead went with their familiar *gh* for these situations, and there are books from the early days of printing that have spellings like *gherle*, *ghes*, *ghoos*, *ghoot*, *ghess*, and *ghest* for *girl*, *geese*, *goose*, *goat*, *guess*, and *guest*.

Those spellings didn't catch on, but *ghost* kept the *h*. Maybe because it looked scarier that way. Indeed, a story about the ghost of a "ghoot gherle ghest" looks downright terrifying.

After a while the *gh* of *ghost* exerted its own spooky power over other words in the same meaning area, like *ghastly* and *aghast*. When the word *ghoul* was borrowed into English in the late 1700s from Arabic, it was at first spelled without the *h*, as *goul* or *goule*. It was later lured to the *gh* group by its meaning similarity to *ghost*.

The *h* managed to attach itself to another, much later word: *gherkin*. The word for the small pickling cucumbers first shows up in the late 1600s as *girkins*, and over the next two hundred years or so is spelled in various ways, including *gurchens*, *gorkems*, and *guerkins* until settling, in the nineteenth century, as *gherkins*. Perhaps it seemed like the right way to spell a word that seemed so Dutch, with its -*kin* ending (even though the Dutch word it came from didn't have the *gh*). Or maybe it just made it seem more like a special, foreign delicacy to compete with the *cornichon*. In any case, the *gh* made the tiny cucumber a bit strange and otherworldly too. Maybe not in a scary way, but there's a fine line between spooky and exciting, scary and intriguing. And a tiny pickled cucumber that looks like a thumb? That's a little ghrisly.

Gnat, Knot, Comb, Wrist

Why Do We Have Silent Consonants?

One of the most noticeable quirks of English spelling is the number of letters that just seem to have no reason to be there at all. The *g* in *gnat*, the *k* in *knot*, the *b* in *comb*, the *w* in *wrist*, the *h* in *why* …Why?

The answer in these cases is pretty straightforward: we used to pronounce them, but now we don't. (In other cases, like *receipt* and *debt*, we never pronounced them. See "Get Receipts on Those Extra Letters.")

The language today has a lot of words where two consonants are said one right after the other with no vowel in between. These consonant clusters, 'sp,' 'tr,' 'fl,' and so on, can be a challenge for speakers of other languages. When Spanish speakers learn English, they tend to break up certain clusters by sticking on a vowel for the first consonant to attach to (so *stop* becomes 'es-top'). Japanese speakers break them up by adding vowels in between (*stop* becomes 'sutoppu').

It's not that English presents a special problem for speakers of other languages. English speakers also make adjustments like this when faced with clusters they aren't used to from other languages, like the 'mb' of Swahili in *mbili* (two), which will come out as 'umbili' or 'muhbuli.' Whether or not a cluster will be difficult to pronounce depends on what you're used to in your own system.

But even when they're part of your system, clusters can be a challenge. Children tend to acquire them later than other aspects of the sound system, and may even keep a cute baby pronunciation like 'pider' for *spider* long after they've mastered most parts of the language. And even among adults who are fully competent native speakers, clusters will be reduced in all kinds of situations. When you say *hands* in a sentence, do you really pronounce the 'd' in there? Are you sure? Whether you perceive it or not, it probably comes out as 'hanz.'

Old English had a whole bunch of consonant clusters that we no longer pronounce. There were words that started with 'hn,' 'hl,' and 'hr' like *hnecca* (neck), *hnutu* (nut), *hleapan* (leap), *hlæder* (ladder), *hrycg* (ridge), and *hrefn* (raven). There were words with 'wl' like *wlispian* (lisp) and *wlæc* (the *luke* of *lukewarm*). These clusters had been completely reduced to 'n,' 'l,' and 'r' by about 1300, long before printing and the standardization of spelling.

There was another group of clusters that look much more familiar to us, because even though we don't pronounce them anymore, they live on in our spelling. The 'wr' of *wrist, wrong,* and *wrath.* The 'kn' of *knot, knit,* and *knee.* The 'gn' of *gnaw* and *gnat,* the 'mb' of *comb* and *lamb,* the 'wh' of *what, where,* and *why.* These were fully pronounced, with both sounds in the cluster, sometimes for hundreds of years after their spellings were established in print. Sometimes, in some dialects, even until today.

For example, a more 'h'-filled version of *wh* words can still be found in parts of Ireland, Scotland, and the United States. The beginning of a word like *where* sounds like the breath of an 'h' coming out through 'w'-formed lips.

Most of the *wh*-spelled words we have were actually originally spelled with *hw* (the first word of the Old English epic poem Beowulf is *hwæt*), but as spelling habits became solidified around using *gh*, *th*, *sh*, and *ch* for various sounds that the Latin alphabet hadn't been designed for, *hw* started to look out of place, and scribes and printers accommodated *hw* to the general pattern by using *wh* instead. The *wh* spelling began to seem so natural and standard that it was even extended to words that had never been spelled or pronounced with a *w*, like *whole* (*hal* in Old English, a relative of *hale* in *hale and hearty*).

Once a pattern with a silent letter settles in, it can exert its own kind of power over other words. Where old words like *comb*, *lamb*, *climb*, and *womb* had their *b*'s from the beginning, *thum*, *crum*, and *lim* did not. People added the *b* onto those words in spelling not because they started pronouncing a 'b' but because it just looked right on the page. And when we borrowed French words like *suc-cumb*, *tomb*, and *bomb*, their *b*'s fit right in whether pronounced or not. The *mb* became just another way to write a final m sound in its own little group of words.

These preserved-in-amber consonants may be silent, but they make a certain kind of life for themselves in the language. If I start to spell my whords whith themb, it whon't look knice, but it whill look like English, and you'll still be able to wread it.

Coulda, Shoulda, Woulda

Why Is There a Silent *L*?

Despite the fact that we tolerate a whole lot of what looks like unsystematic randomness in English, we often end up shaping that disorder into order in small ways over time. In the case of *could/would/should*, a soothingly consistent group, we evened things out by adjusting a spelling. We added an *l*, one of those frustrating silent letters that didn't need to be there, and we did it just to make that little group more harmonious.

We added the silent *l* to *could*, which came from the *l*-less verb *can*, meaning "to know how to" or "to have the ability to." The past tense of *can* was *cuthe*, and then *coude*, and that became *could*. The *l* was already in *should* and *would*, but, in contrast to the *could* case, it made sense for it to be there. *Shulde* was the past tense of *shall*, and *wolde* was the past tense of *will*, and the *l* in those words used to be pronounced.

But *l*'s before other consonants have a way of avoiding being pronounced, either by being absorbed into the vowel that comes before it, transforming its quality, or leaving the scene entirely. Some *l*'s in this position in Old English dropped out long before the advent of printing and spelling standardization. For example, *which*, *each*, and *such* all once had *l*'s before their final consonants as *hwilc*, *aelc*, and *swilc*. But other *l*'s stuck it out to become immortalized in spelling long after no one was pronouncing them anymore.

If the *l* of *should* and *would* were still being reliably pronounced in the sixteenth century, it would have been strange to start writing it in *could* where there had never been an '1.' But since it was already the case that *l* was usually silent, the *could* spelling could fit in naturally.

But why change it at all? There was a similarity in the way the words were being used, not just as past tenses of *can*, *will*, and *shall* but to express a stance toward a statement: it's possible (*could*); it's conditional (*would*); it's advisable (*should*). They seemed three of a kind, and so in a sense going together that way as a neat team, they all got the team jacket. An *-ould* spelling.

There are other words with silent *l*'s that were once pronounced, like *walk*, from the Old English *wealcan*, and *talk*, which is related to *tell* with an old suffix on the end. *Stalk*, related to *steal*, had the same suffix. Some people would argue that these *l*'s aren't silent at all, that when they speak, they actually pronounce them. But it can be hard to tell the difference between a vowel followed by an 'l' sound and a slightly different quality vowel. Is *yolk* the same as *yoke* for you? Is *balm* the same as *bomb*? If not, is it because the 'l' sound is actually there, or is the vowel just different?

An *l* in the spelling can have a powerful effect on how we hear or pronounce a word. There are a number of words that we got from French without any *l* and left them that way for a long time. The word *fault*, for example, was first used in English the French way, as *faut*. But in the 1500s, when Latinizing was all the rage (see "Blame the Snobs"; "Get Receipts on Those Extra Letters"), people started writing it as *fault*, to make the etymological connection to *fallere*. They still pronounced it 'faut,' though—in works of the seventeenth century it is rhymed with *thought* and *wrought*. Eventually, though, the spelling influenced the pronunciation, and we started saying the 'l' sound. The same thing happened to *assault* and *falcon*, which were originally *assaut* and *faucon*.

During this Latinizing phase, *l* was added to other words where it still doesn't get pronounced, like *salmon*. But spelling may be having its effect here too. In some places people *do* say the 'l' sound in salmon, or at least insist they do.

*L*s are tricky. In some environments they can become very vowel-like and retain just enough ambiguity that it's unclear whether they're there or not. But in certain words, like *would* and *should*, it's clear that they went silent long ago, and in *could*, that they never had anything to say at all.

Peek, Peak, Piece, People

Why Are There So Many Ways to Write the 'Ee' Sound?

Ugh, vowels! Vowels are so slippery, so changeable, so hard to define simply. We use terms like open, closed, long, or short to give an idea of what vowels sound like, but they hardly tell you anything at all. The best we can do is turn to rhymes. I can tell you that in the fifteenth century the vowel in *meet* was more like the one in today's *mate*. But that's assuming my own midwestern American pronunciation. It wasn't at all like the Australian pronunciation of *mate*, which to my American ear sounds like *mite*.

Consonants also change and vary from time to time and place to place, but they are much easier to get a handle on. They are more definable. A consonant is caused by an obstruction of some kind. For a 'p' sound the obstruction is the lips coming together. For a 't' sound it is the tongue meeting the ridge behind the teeth. For a 'k' sound it is the back of the tongue meeting the soft palate. There are plenty of other things that go into the quality of a particular consonant, but it's possible to describe them with specific, concrete details of how they're made.

For vowels, there is no obstruction, only a subtle shaping of the air. The body of the tongue raises and lowers and goes back and forth. The lips round and unround. The sound bends slightly; sometimes it matters (a *pin* is not a *pen*), and sometimes it doesn't (if you live in the American South, a *pin* is still not a *pen*, but you might pronounce them exactly the same).

The shifting indeterminacy of vowels is not a problem of English but of language in general. There are many writing systems for other languages that don't even bother to use symbols for vowels, so that shifting doesn't mess with spelling traditions. It does mess with spelling for English, but not simply because we try to write them down. Other languages that use the same alphabet as we do are more dependable in how their vowels are represented.

There are spelling inconsistencies for all the vowels in English, but things really get out of control for the 'ee' sound. There are just so many ways to write it in English. One *e* (*me*), two *e*'s (*beer*), an *ie* (*believe*), an *ea* (*leaf*), an *ei* (*seize*), an *i* (*police*), a *y* (*messy*), an *ey* (*key*), a *ui* (*mosquito*), an *eo* (*people*), and even an *oe* (*phoenix*).

The stripped-down, simplified story is this: Many of the words that today have the 'ee' sound used to have a different vowel sound. There was a sound closer to 'ey' spelled *e* in words like *me* (approx. 'mey'), a slightly different sound spelled *eo* in words like *beor* (*beer*, approx. 'beyuhr'), and another sound spelled *ea* in words like *leaf* (approx. 'leyahf,' but kind of rhymes with *laugh* in the American pronunciation . . . keep in mind, these approximations are terrible. Once again, ugh, vowels!).

You might say, when it comes to vowels, we're speaking modern English and writing late medieval English, but that wouldn't be quite right. The pronunciation changed, but so did the writing system. At first they changed together, but in kind of a haphazard way. Different scribes had different habits for representing the vowels they heard around them, and because of dialect differences, they heard different things. To take just one example, the word *ear* was at different times spelled *eare*, *eir*, *er*, *eyre*, *eer*, *yre*, *ir*, *ar*, or *aeir*. The different spellings sometimes represent dialect differences and sometimes varying scribal habits for how to show the same sound.

When the printing press arrived, the variation continued, but more texts could be produced, and they could spread more widely. And those texts brought spellings with them that more people absorbed, learned, got used to, and taught others. If you said *speak* as 'speek' and a few towns to the west they said it as 'spake,' you could all still get accustomed to the *s-p-e-a-k* spelling as representing your pronunciation.

It took some time, but standards developed for how things should be spelled. Printed material encouraged the developing standards for how things should be written, even though there were always dialect differences in how they were pronounced. This happened for languages all over Europe; a written standard emerged for Spanish, German, French, and so on, even when there was a lot of variation in spoken dialects.

But English became the victim of some really bad timing. Over the same couple of centuries that the printing press was standardizing and entrenching our spelling habits, the vowel system was undergoing a massive reorganization, which we now refer to as the Great Vowel Shift.

Many words we have today were pronounced very differently before the fourteenth century. *Boot* sounded more 'like boat,' *house* sounded like 'hoos,' and *five* sounded like 'feev.' Over the course of the fourteenth and fifteenth centuries, words with long vowels shifted into new pronunciations. They took over vowel spaces that were already occupied by other words and pushed them into new positions, and the displaced vowels, in turn, pushed their neighbors out to diphthong land.

The changes may have been initiated by the volume of French words that entered English shortly before the shift, or by the movement of populations with different dialects during the Black Plague, but when they were complete, the language sounded quite different, and spelling was a mess, since many spellings had been established during earlier phases of pronunciation.

If the sound changes had been completed or were at least further along when the rise of printing started to stabilize spelling, we may have been left with a more predictable writing system. If the spelling had been established before the massive sound changes took place, we may have had a system that didn't match the way we actually spoke but had more internal consistency (like French, with its many silent letters and alternate vowel spellings but relatively few outright surprises).

As it happened, we hit the perfect storm on an already choppy sea. See?

Crew, Grew, Stew, New ... Sew?

Why Don't *Sew* and *New* Rhyme?

Sew looks like it should rhyme with *new*. And *crew* and *grew* and *knew/flew/dew/few/blew/stew/nephew/curfew/view* ... whew! But it doesn't.

It's a well-known and complained-about fact that English has pairs of words that look like they should rhyme but don't. *How* does not rhyme with *low*. But both words have teams of fellow words that share their patterns and offer support for their spelling-pronunciation case. *How* has *cow*, *now*, and *plow*. *Low* has *snow*, *flow*, and *grow*. *Speak* and *steak* don't rhyme, but *speak* has *peak*, *weak*, *freak*, *beak*, and *leak*, and while *steak* only has *break* on its side, it has another team supporting the *ea* spelling of its vowel in *great* and *yea*.

But *sew*? While *new* has enough buddies to fill a stadium, *sew* has nobody. Nobody but the slight variations of its own self in *sewn* and *sewer*, and even there Team New butts in by making the word for "a person who sews" look like a drainage system for waste. No wonder people overwhelmingly went with *seamstress* instead.

If you really dig, it is possible to unearth some faint, historical connections to the spelling of *sew*. The English town of Shrewsbury offers a clue. There has been a long-standing debate, even among born and bred residents, about the proper pronunciation of the name of the town. Is it 'shrowzbree' or 'shroozbree'? Depends who you ask.

English place names, with their charmingly counterintuitive spellings (*Worcester* is 'wooster'?) are a notoriously bad source for untangling sound-spelling relationships. Even so, residents usually agree on one preferred pronunciation, even when it veers wildly from what you'd expect. Cholmondeley is 'chumlee.' Belvoir is 'beaver.' If you don't pronounce it right, it marks you as an out-of-towner, not as someone with another valid preference. But Shrewsbury can't get consensus.

Shrewsbury as 'shrowzbree' cannot just be chalked up to the principle of Delightfully Eccentric English Place Names. There was a time in its history when there was more widespread back-and-forth in words with 'ew' and 'ow.' For example, the verb we now know only as *show* was commonly spelled as *shew* well into the nineteenth century. It was also pronounced as 'shew.' We know this because of literature in verse where it is rhymed with words like *view* and *true*.

Strew also showed this alternation (in some dialects today, things can be "strown about"), and so did *shrew*, the little animal (and by figurative extension the ill-tempered nag), which shows up with the spellings *shrowe*, *shro*, and *shrow*.

Sew was often spelled *sow*, as it was in both the King James Bible (Job 14:17, "My transgression is sealed vp in a bagge, and thou sowest vp mine iniquitie"), and in Shakespeare (Ophelia in *Hamlet*: "As I was sowing in my closet"). But it was also the case that in other works *sew* was rhymed with *clue* and *new*.

Two things were happening in the sixteenth through nineteenth centuries. Pronunciation of some words was varying between a *shrew* vowel and a *show* vowel, and spelling was varying between an *ew* and an *ow*. It's not always the case that they varied in coordination with each other. As we know from rhymed verse, a word might be spelled with *ew* and pronounced as 'ow.' This is precisely where *sew* landed and settled down.

But why did none of the others end up there? Everyone else—*show*, *strew*, *shrew*—settled into a pronunciation and a spelling that matched. Except for Shrewsbury, which still hasn't made up its mind.

It might have been that *sew* had a competitor, *sow* (as in "to plant seeds"), another verb that it had to distinguish itself from through spelling. It didn't have to worry about *sow*, the pig, because that's a noun and therefore unlikely to enter into any sentence structure where it could sow confusion. It could have distinguished itself through pronunciation, but that would put it in conflict with the verb *sue*.

Of course, nothing in English spelling history is ever that simple, and until the seventeenth century, *sue* was often spelled as *sew*. But it seems that by then, the pronunciations of both were well established, and it eventually came to the point where all three verbs had three different spellings. *Sow, sew, sue*.

It may not seem like it, but there is a backward, stumbling-into-it way that the spelling system optimizes itself over time. There are many, many instances of words that sound the same but mean different things and are spelled differently *(hear/here, tail/tale)*. Or words that are spelled the same but mean different things and are pronounced differently (*wound* as in *wound up*, *wound* as in *bandaged wound*).

On the face of it, this seems like the worst optimization job ever. But it is very, very rare for two words to have the same pronunciation and spelling AND be the same part of speech unless one of them derives from the other. *Bark* is a noun in its tree sense and a verb in its dog sense. You CAN have the noun "a dog's bark," but that's derived from the verb and still very unlikely to show up in the same contexts as the other noun. Some other verb-noun pairs using the same sound and spelling are *bear, duck, rock, tire,* and *saw.*

Sew and *sow*, as two words with different, unrelated meanings and the same pronunciation that were also both verbs that could be placed in similar sentence contexts, found their way to different spellings. Not because any authority declared it or planned it but because of the haphazard yet self-organizing way individual decisions by writers or printers accumulated into a habit that would make the meaning a little clearer.

Blame the Snobs

After the printing press started churning out books, English began to flourish as a written language. It had been dormant for a long time, shoved aside by French and Latin in domains where people wrote things down. So while it was robust and healthy as a spoken language, there was no trusted authority or tradition to follow when writing it. That wasn't such a problem at first, but soon people felt the need for some direction, some standardizing influence.

In the sixteenth century English was felt to be deficient compared to Latin and Greek, which learned people still studied in school. However, most of the growing reading public wanted books in English. Authors obliged but often prefaced their English works with defensive justifications for why they were writing in English and apologies for how, as one translation noted, "our grosse tongue is a rude and a barren tong."

The movement away from classical languages brought about a corresponding movement to bring the rude and barren tongue up to snuff with some conscious attention. Scholars working on translations of the classics were frustrated that there were "many wordes in Latyn that we haue no proper englyssh according therto" (as the translator of a devotional for nuns wrote in 1530). The solution was to enrich the vocabulary with Latin. They borrowed and cobbled together new words from Latin parts. Words like *describe, deduce, explain,* and *illustrate* were (to use a few more of the new coinages) *introduced, incorporated,* and *accepted.*

But things started to get out of hand. They also came up with plenty of words that have since faded away: words like *suppeditation* (the act of supplying), *illecebrous* (enticing), *allaqueate* (ensnared), and *addubitation* (the act of questioning oneself). These types of creations caused some backlash, earning a mocking nickname: "inkhorn terms," after the portable ink containers, originally made from animal horn, that scholars hung from their belts.

The backlash also included some attempts to translate using native English word stock instead. One scholar, in his attempt to bring Aristotle's logical principles to an English audience, rendered the "art of reason" as *witcraft* and *conclusion, negation,* and *definition* as *endsay, naysay,* and *saywhat.* But those kinds of attempts petered out. The classical languages exerted too much power, and there was too much insecurity about the worthiness of the vernacular.

By the eighteenth century the vernacular had proved itself worthy. Being educated came to mean familiarity not just with Aristotle, Cicero, and Virgil but also with Locke, Milton, and Shakespeare. English could handle big, intellectual ideas, but the idea of correct language, when it came to spelling or grammar, was still flexible.

It wouldn't stay that way. In 1712 Jonathan Swift wrote *A Proposal for Correcting, Improving, and Ascertaining the English Tongue* (with *ascertain* having the sense "to make definite, to fix"). In his opinion, English rose to its highest form during the Elizabethan era, had a few good decades, and then started going downhill. He suggested that an academy should be established to settle the proper rules of English. He didn't say what the rules should be, but he did have some specific complaints about what people shouldn't be doing—mostly shortening too many words, like using *mob* for the Latin term for a disorderly crowd, *mobile vulgus*, and *disturb'd* for *disturbed* (which should have three syllables).

While Italian and French already had language academies at this time, and more would be formed for other languages, the English Academy never came to be. But that didn't stop the complaints from coming. Writers of dictionaries and grammars in the eighteenth century objected to *had rather*, *had better*, and the use of *noways* for *nowise*. For the first time these writers drew an explicit distinction between *lay* and *lie*, and a preference was expressed for *different from* over *different to*. These preferences, as they were repeated, coalesced into rules, or rather, prescriptions. Not descriptions of what people did, but descriptions of what they should do.

This way of creating a language standard for English was purposeful, unlike the first wave of standardization, which had happened organically. In the fourteenth through seventeenth centuries, when someone sat down to write in English, they were influenced by all the things they had read in English. They reproduced some of the spellings or phrasing they had seen, sometimes imperfectly, but reproduced nonetheless. The more any particular habit of writing passed from one person to another, the more it would be read and go on to influence the habits of others. Pretty soon, certain ways of writing started to seem recognizable and normal and others to seem unfamiliar or wrong.

But not everywhere in every domain on the same schedule. These emerging standards differed from region to region and depended on which domain of writing was doing the influencing (court reports? sermons? recipes?). If a person wanted to know the *correct* spelling or the *correct* phrasing, there was no general authority to turn to.

The whole idea that there was a "correctness" to aim for in English developed slowly but really took off in the eighteenth century. It was the age of etiquette and the codification of social rules. There were now self-styled general authorities for all kinds of things. You could buy guides to "good deportment," "good manners," and "genteel behavior." And pretty soon there were books on good language too.

The first major dictionary of English, Samuel Johnson's dictionary of 1755, was published during this time, and it became a source of authority for spelling. Robert Lowth's 1762 *Short Introduction to English Grammar* went through more than twenty editions, and some of his complaints, such as that *whose* should be used for people and not for things, were copied in the thousands of advice books that followed. (So no to "The *question*, *whose* solution I require / Is what the sex of women most desire." Sorry, Dryden.)

But the advice books and newspaper columns on language usage that followed in the nineteenth century were more extreme in their pronouncements. Where Lowth had said in a footnote, "*Whose* is by some authors made the possessive case of *which*, and applied to things as well as persons; I think, improperly," future authors recast mild statements of opinion like this as hard rules. The new grammars were collections of all the terrible mistakes you might be making. And they were not just called "mistakes" but "perversions," "vulgarities," "revolting," "barbarisms," "ridiculous," "abominations," "laughable," and "absurd."

In this environment of very public, and intentionally hu-
miliating, language monitoring, a cloud of insecurity developed
and perpetuated itself. People who had been berated for specific
aspects of language use went on to berate others. Those who had
internalized non-obvious enforced distinctions like the difference
between *done* and *finished*, or *masterly* and *masterful*, or *more than*
and *over*, or *fix* and *repair* continued to insist on those distinctions
long after even prestigious publications no longer enforced them.

This is a book about standard English. There is no need to look
to nonstandard dialects or lists of "common mistakes" or "things
everyone gets wrong" to talk about what's highly irregular or weird
about English. It should be clear by now that the standard—
the "correct," authorized version—is unsystematic and illogical enough on its own. Some of that is the result of the natural

accumulation of historical forces, but some of it comes from intentional meddling.

I use the term *snobs* for the ones who did the meddling. It has bad connotations. Snobs think too highly of themselves. They look down on people. They care too much about social class. They aim to impress. Not all of the people involved in the decisions that led to the issues in this section displayed all of those characteristics. Some were just making decisions where a decision needed to be made. Sometimes those decisions were later wielded as social weapons by true snobs.

This doesn't mean that standards are bad. Standards are good to have! Whether or not the intentions of anyone involved were good or bad, casual or judgmental, when a standard emerges, it becomes the standard. Writers, publishers, editors, and teachers need to have a basis for consistency in what they do, and having an agreed-upon set of rules for how to spell things, how to form sentences, what words mean, is useful. But standards can change, and when they do, it can feel like some supreme law of truth and logic is being violated.

That's just not the case. The standards themselves did not emerge from supreme laws of truth and logic but from people doing stuff, sometimes out of snobbery, oftentimes irrationally and inconsistently.

In this section I cover some of the stuff they did—how snobs, and a certain insecurity about English, led to difficult-to-learn spellings ("Get Receipts on Those Extra Letters"; "Asthma, Phlegm, and Diarrhea") and an aping of the grammatical rules of more prestigious languages ("The Data Are In on the Octopi"). They made individual decisions about whether meanings were different enough to make one word with related senses or two completely different words ("Too Much Discretion"). They linked language to patriotic sentiment and created rules to promote that sentiment ("Pick a Color/Colour"). Some of those actions were passed on to be used by snobs and non-snobs alike, but that doesn't mean they had the supreme rules of truth and logic at their command.

Get Receipts on Those Extra Letters

Why Is There a *P* in *Receipt*, an *L* in *Salmon*, and a *B* in *Doubt*?

Silent consonants got into English in a few ways. One group of them, the *gnat-comb-wrist-should* kind, was there in the beginning and simply kept hanging around after we stopped pronouncing them. Another group, the *pneumatic-psychiatric-mnemonic* kind, came in with scholarly words coined or borrowed by scholarly people using spellings from scholarly classical languages. A similar group, words of the *rendezvous–faux pas–gnocchi* type, were borrowed with their fancy continental spellings and maintained to display their fancy foreign origins.

Most silent consonants belong to one of those groups, but there is another group: silent consonants that were not there when they became English but were added later to emphasize their high-class origins.

Receipt, *salmon*, and *doubt* came into English through French and were at first spelled in various ways that approximated how they were pronounced. *Receipt* (*recette* in modern French) might be *receit*, *resayt*, or *recyte*. *Salmon* (*saumon* in modern French) could be *samoun*, *samowne*, or *samon*. *Doubt* (*doute* in modern French) was spelled *doute*, *dote*, or even *doughte* in old texts.

If you were in the know—well-educated and familiar with Latin—you could see that these words traced back to the Latin words that had developed into the French words over the previous centuries. The related Latin words, *receptus*, *salmo*, and *dubitare*, had some extra consonants in them, but they had stopped being pronounced in French and weren't pronounced or written in English.

But they could be! If you wanted to play up your familiarity with those classical origins, you could stick them back in. During the Renaissance, writers and translators started using more and more Latin words in order to enrich the vocabulary or just show off. They borrowed words straight from Latin like *receptive* and *dubious*. And older words that were distant relatives of those were recast in a Latin mold. *Receipt* gained a *p*, *doubt* gained a *b*, and salmon got its *l*.

They weren't the only ones. *Dette* became *debt*. *Endite* became *indict*. In most cases, the Latin-inspired interloper letters remained silent, but sometimes putting them back in writing made literate people eventually start pronouncing them too. *Perfect* first entered English in the *c*-less French way, as *parfit*. In the late sixteenth century the Latin connection to *perfectus* was made explicit in the spelling, but it wasn't until much later that people started to actually pronounce the *c*. Even a hundred years later it was often pronounced as *perfet*. Something similar happened to *adventure*, which came in as *aventure*, and *falcon*, which was long pronounced *faucon*.

In a few cases, the urge to Latinize spellings made etymological connections that were never there in the first place. *Iland*, for example, was from an Old English word, *ígland*, but in the late sixteenth century it gained an *s* to become *island* on the mistaken assumption that it had something to do with Latin *insula*. Likewise *sithe*, from an Old English word for a cutting implement, became *scythe* on the assumption that it had some connection to the Latin *scindere*, for cut (which is a valid root in the word *rescind*). *Scissors* (formerly *sisours*) also got its *c* from a mistaken *scindere* assumption.

Latinized spelling was haphazardly applied and didn't always stick. While *receipt* held on to its mute *p*, *deceit* could have just as well become *deceipt*, but though a few writers tried that out, it didn't take. Other Latinized forms like *sainct* for *saint* (better to see the *sanctus*) and *hable* for *able* (connecting it back to *habilis*) also died on the vine.

So we're left with silent letters that only sometimes give us a little peek at the distant history of words and where we got them. We did get a lot of words from Latin, but sometimes we forged the receipts.

Asthma, Phlegm, and Diarrhea

Why All the Extra Letters?

Medicine is a scientific profession with a lot of fancy words. We know to expect that workaday aches, pains, and bodily problems will have other, special, and difficult technical names in professional situations. Pinkeye is *conjunctivitis*, a sore throat *pharyngitis*, an ingrown toenail *onchocryptosis*. Most words like these were coined relatively recently, in the nineteenth century, during the establishment of modern medicine, from Latin and Greek roots.

But Latin and Greek had already gotten themselves into English much earlier than that in a less obvious way. The previous waves of Latin/Greek influence look more like the rest of English and don't stand out so much. You can see the difference in the development of the ways we talk about guts. *Guts* was there first. It comes from the Old English word for all that stuff inside our midsection. After the French arrived, we got a new word, *entrails*, which was our version of the French *entraille*, which was their version, ultimately, of the Latin *interanea*. A few hundred years later, in the eighteenth century, when people writing medical texts looked directly to Latin sources for vocabulary inspiration, we acquired an even fancier word, *viscera*.

Early-borrowed words like *fever* (Latin *febris*), *vomit* (Latin *vomitus*), and *pus* (Latin *pus*, Greek *pous*) look completely natural in English, while their later-borrowed counterparts, *pyrexia*, *regurgitation*, and *suppuration*, seem like they're trying a little too hard to not look like English at all. Between those extremes are words like *exhale*, *intestine*, and *indigestion*—pretty normal, not trying too hard, but they definitely have a Latin look about them. *Indigestion* apparently settled into English so well that it became too mundane; the cool, classical-language trendsetters of the eighteenth century turned to Greek to pull out a more impressive *dyspepsia*.

Asthma, *phlegm*, and *diarrhea* (or *diarrhoea* in British spelling) have a *pharyngitis* or *dyspepsia* look about them, with all those strange extra letters, but they aren't like those pretentious newcomers. They all came into English with the early wave. They began their English careers in the fourteenth century, but they began as *asma, fleume,* and *diaria.*

It wasn't as if English didn't have any concept of those things before that. Old English had words like *angbreost* ("tight chest"), *horh* ("phlegm, mucus"), and *unryne* ("ill running"), but like many words from the old Germanic layer, they were replaced as French poured in and the vocabulary changed. Even so, at this early stage there was still usually an attempt to spell things as they were pronounced.

Later, after the printing press made the mass production of texts possible, classical works were printed and circulated both in the original and in translation. People familiar with the spellings of the classical sources started to change the spellings of words in order to show their etymology. Words like *receipt* and *doubt* were Latinized (see "Get Receipts on Those Extra Letters"), and words like *asthma, phlegm,* and *diarrhea* were Greek-ified.

Of course, when words were Greek-ified, they weren't taken all the way back to Greek spellings in the Greek alphabet, but rather to the Latin-alphabet spelling conventions for Greek. Greek letters like theta (θ), phi (φ), and chi (χ) originally represented "aspirated" consonants in ancient Greek, basically, 't,' 'p,' and 'k,' but with an extra puff of air, so they were spelled in Latin as *th, ph,* and *ch.* Rho was also aspirated at the beginning of words and prefixed word roots and was spelled as *rh* in Latin in those cases. The vowel diphthongs *αι* and *οι* were written as *æ* and *œ* (*diphthong* itself being a strange-looking English word from a Greek word with a phi and a theta in the middle).

The *g* of *phlegm* was never pronounced in English except in related words where the *m* could attach to another syllable, like *phlegmatic* (originally *fleumatike*). Later borrowings like *enigma* and *stigma* were borrowed straight from Greek (or from Greek via Latin) and came with the end syllable already in place; there was never an earlier *enim* or *stim* to establish a 'g'-less pronunciation like *fleume* had. Otherwise we might have *enigm* and *stigm* to write about.

The turn toward the display of Greek etymology was particularly strong for medical terms. *Catar, rewme, emerardes,* and *colera* became *catarrh, rheum, haemorrhoids,* and *cholera. Stomak* became *stomach. Farmacie* became *pharmacy.* But these kinds of spelling changes can be found throughout the vocabulary. *Quire* became *choir, caracter* became *character. Fesant* and *fenix* became *pheasant* and *phoenix.*

These words were made more difficult to spell on purpose. But it wasn't done with malice. It was done with an eye toward elevating the language, linking it back to a glorious ancient source. And you have to admit, it does make asthma, phlegm, and diarrhea seem just a tad more dignified.

The Data Are In on the Octopi

What's the Deal with Latin Plurals?

Is it "the data *are* in" or "the data *is* in"? *Octopi*, *octopuses*, or *octopodes*? For the grammatical treatment of plural and Latin/Greek derived words, how did we get these competing formulas? Formulae?

Words with unusual Latin or Greek plural forms are indeed English, but they haven't fully committed. Other irregular plurals in the language—*children*, *oxen*, *mice*, *teeth*—reflect older patterns in the language. They got their plural forms through regular English processes a long time ago when those processes were still active, and they just stayed that way. But words with Latin- and Greek-style plurals aren't old at all. Well, the words themselves are old—they come from ancient languages, after all—but they were brought into English in the modern era. Most of the time they follow modern rules (*schemas*, *enigmas*, and *stadiums* do just fine for *schemata*, *enigmata*, and *stadia*), but sometimes they don't (*alumni*, *nuclei*). For some words this state of affairs leaves us all confused.

English has a long relationship with Latin, going all the way back to before English was even a language. The Germanic tribes that eventually settled in Britain had already borrowed words like *street* (*strata*), *cheese* (*caesus*), and *wine* (*vinum*). After those tribes settled down and started to speak the beginnings of English, the missionaries who brought Christianity to Britain also brought words like *altar* (*altare*), *candle* (*candela*), *bishop* (*episcopus*), and *priest* (*presbyter*).

These early words were naturalized, incorporated, and adapted to English pronunciation and grammar. The plural of *candle* became *candles*; no one tried to make it *candelae*. A feast was a *feast* and not a *festum*.

Then more Latin came in after the Norman conquest in the form of the French words that were themselves derived from Latin words. Words also came directly from Latin, as it served as the written language of official institutions. These were incorporated too. We got *numbers, poems,* and *paradoxes,* not *numeri, poemata,* and *paradoxa*.

That changed with the Renaissance, an age of science and scholarship. The printing press had made wide distribution of classical texts possible. Translations from Latin often left Latin terms as they were and had people reading in English about the classification of the natural world into *genera* and *species,* not *genuses* and *specieses*. Works on medicine, philosophy, and rhetoric introduced other terms and their fancy plurals.

People got familiar with fancy plurals from their reading or their education, but there wasn't really a culture of insistence that there was one correct way to use them in English. In the seventeenth and eighteenth centuries you could write about "collecting datas" and not be attacked by a flood of letters to the editor about your mistake. Highly educated people wrote *funguses, focuses, genuses,* and even *specieses* without losing any credibility.

That began to change in the nineteenth century. That culture of insistence that there was one correct way I just mentioned? It sprouted, grew to enormous size, and took over. The publication of grammar books exploded (see "Blame the Snobs"), and the books were huge sellers. Where early books of this type had outlined "how good writers use language," they turned into strongly worded lists of "Don't do this." Readers licked their chops looking forward to delicious takedowns in newspaper columns on language errors. Teachers began to take points off for *data is*. Knuckles began to be rapped for *genuses*.

In this environment two things developed with respect to Latin/Greek plurals: an insecurity about how to use them and a corresponding show-offy overcompensation. If you want to talk about more than one octopus, you'll hesitate before saying *octopuses*, thinking, "Does that sound ignorant?" So you go for *octopi*, thinking, "Aha, clever me, I have recognized a Latin root without ever having gotten my knuckles rapped for it." Then you proudly criticize others for saying *octopuses*.

This kind of overcompensation led to even more harrumphy lists of errors, magazine columns on mistaken formations like *ignorami* ("*Ignoramus* is not a noun in Latin!"), *magnum opi* ("The plural of *opus* is *opera*!"), and *hiati* ("Fourth declension! The plural is *hiatus*!"). These responses display a certain luxurious pleasure in complaining about how wrong other people were while simultaneously showcasing a superior knowledge of classical languages.

The one-upmanship complaint about *octopi* was that the -*us* of *octopus* does not represent the noun suffix that becomes -*i* in the plural but just the coincidentally matching last two letters of the Latin rendering of the Greek word for foot, *pous*. Therefore the truly correct plural should use the Greek rules, so *octopodes*. And while we're at it, have you heard about *platypodes* and *rhinocerotes*?

Today, *octopodes*, *platypodes*, and *rhinocerotes* are only said in joking performances of dramatic pedantry. *Octopuses* is perfectly fine English, but many people find it hard to say with confidence. There's still a hesitation, a reflex of the ingrained bodily memory of the flinch before the knuckle rap.

Data (originally the plural of *datum*) is now more often used with singular verb agreement. It is a mass noun, like *evidence* or *information*, and it's been used that way for a long time. Still, style guides continue to pass down a caution about its use, a warning that you might be challenged on "the data is," and it's good preparation to know why.

The flinch before the use of the Latin plural need no longer be caused by insecurity about whether you're correct or not but by the expectation that no matter how confident you are that you are not making an ignorant mistake, the great-great-great-grandstudents of the nineteenth-century fashionable scolding grammar books are still out there judging you.

Too Much Discretion
Keeping *Discreet* and *Discrete* Discrete, Discreetly

There are so many homophones in English! They sound the same; they're spelled differently; how are we supposed to keep track? There's a whole industry built around lists of common errors and mistakes to watch out for, and they always include a bunch of easily confused homophones: *accept* and *except*, *here* and *hear*, *your* and *you're*, and of course *there*, *their*, and *they're* (just to name a few).

In many cases, we ended up with these pairs (or triplets) because of the luck (or bad fortune) of natural sound changes. Different words that used to be pronounced differently came to be pronounced the same through changes that happened over time, or words got fused together in contractions in a way that just happened to match an existing word. The dreaded *there*, *their*, *they're* triple suffered from both types of bad luck, plus an additional one—they are used with similar frequency. No one puts *I'll* and *aisle*, *weave* and *we've*, or *heed* and *he'd* on their "errors to watch out for" lists, because the members of those pairs are never competing with each other.

Discreet and *discrete*, however, do compete with each other, and are easily confused. But they did not get that way through sound changes. They are, in fact, the same word, or were in any event, but we ended up spelling them differently. And not even that long ago.

They both go back to the Latin *discretus*, for "separate" or "distinct." We use the *discrete* spelling for this sense now. One of the popular techniques for getting students to remember this is to point out that the two *e*'s in *discrete* are being separated by the *t*. Its other meaning, the one we spell *discreet*, comes through the idea of having the good judgment to know the best way to separate things out: being *discerning*, having *discretion*.

That was the main sense of the word when it first came into English from the French. *Discreet*, which was also spelled *discrete*, *discrett*, *discreyt*, *dyscrite*, or *discreate*, meant prudent, tactful, unobtrusive.

In the sixteenth century, scholarly works in areas like mathematics and logic began to use the word in its more technical "separate" *discretus* sense. It was usually spelled *discrete*, along the same lines as other Latin terms being introduced during this phase like *obsolete*, *complete*, and *concrete*. But it wasn't necessarily perceived as a completely different word, much in the way that we can think of *certain* in its "absolutely sure" sense (I am certain I gave it to you) or its "some particular but unspecified" sense (certain people never learn) while perceiving them as the same word. We could have decided to spell one of them *sertin* and ended up with two different words.

Well into the nineteenth century the *Webster's Dictionary* entry for *discreet* included the following note: "Sometimes written *discrete*; the distinction between *discreet* and *discrete* is arbitrary, but perhaps not entirely useless."

"Arbitrary, but perhaps not entirely useless" is a long way from the current view that these are totally different words that you'd be a fool to confuse. But it doesn't matter what they used to be. According to our instituted language standards now, they are indeed different words, spelled differently.

They got to be this way through conscious choices, decided somewhat arbitrarily and then passed down until they had the force of law. What was a preference became a rule.

One person, if they have enough authority, can turn their own preference into a rule. The word pronounced *travel*, for example, once had two related meanings, "to exert oneself in work" and "to make a long journey" (which was a type of hard work and exertion). Samuel Johnson, in his massively influential 1755 dictionary, split the senses into two spellings, *travail* and *travel*, noting that "in some writers the word is written alike in all its senses; but it is more convenient to write *travail* for labour, and *travel* for journey."

At the time of Johnson's dictionary the words were pronounced the same. It was later that the pronunciation of *travail* changed to rhyme with *avail*, under pressure from the spelling. *Travail* and *travel* became completely different words.

Who decided *discreet* and *discrete* should be different words? No one person in particular, but it became a way for scholarly types to emphasize the more Latin sense in their more technical use of the word, distinguishing it from the common way most people used it.

Specialist fields develop their own vocabulary because they don't want their specific concepts confused with more general, everyday concepts. This happens all the time, but it doesn't always result in a homophone. For example, though we already had the word *scheme*, philosophers introduced *schema* to mean something more specific. We already had *monotonous*, but writers in music and mathematics needed *monotonic*.

In many cases, though, it does result in a homophone. *Council/counsel* and *ensure/insure* were made separate through specialization to professional contexts. And there are tendencies distinguishing the same word in different fields that haven't quite reached the status of rules. *Aesthetics* is more common in the domains of art and philosophy, while *esthetics* is more common in the beauty business. *Analogue* goes with literature, while *analog* goes with electronics, at least in US usage.

The assigning of tiny spelling distinctions to different domains can take on importance in showing off specialized knowledge. If you're in the know, you spell *whiskey* with an *e* if it's Irish or

American and *whisky* without an *e* if its Scotch, Canadian, or Japanese whisky. The fact that there are two spellings becomes almost a test: a test of how well-versed you are in the conventions of the spirits industry.

Getting the difference between *discreet* and *discrete* is a similar kind of test, but on a larger scale: a test of how well versed you are in the conventions of English. Even if you have been steeped in those conventions all your life, you may still have to stop and think for a moment to remember the rule and pass the test.

Pick a Color/Colour
Can't We Get This Standardized/Standardised?

Should you organize your shirts by color or organise them by colour? Generally speaking, *organize* and *color* are American spellings, and *organise* and *colour* are British. It's bad enough we have to learn one crazy English spelling system, but now you're telling me there are two?

Yes, but fortunately they don't differ by too much. For a limited set of words, there are alternate spellings that are usually defined as US or UK spellings and will have varying usage in Canada, Australia, and other Commonwealth nations. The good news is that if you use either alternative, it won't technically be wrong, but it may rub your audience the wrong way. *Pyjamas* is the standard UK spelling, and *pajamas* is the standard US spelling, but if you swap one for the other for the wrong audience, it only looks somewhat strange. Not wrong in the way *pidgeamehs* would be.

It makes sense that borrowed words like *pajamas/pyjamas* would end up with alternate spellings. When we adopt a word from another language (especially one with a different writing system), we have to figure out how we're going to represent it. Is a Russian emperor a *tsar* or a *czar*? Is the Korean fermented cabbage dish *kimchee* or *kimchi*? *Pajamas* was borrowed in the nineteenth century from an Urdu-Persian source. Early spellings of it included *piejamahs* and *pigammahs*. Those are both nonstandard now. *Pajamas* and *pyjamas* are both standard, just in different places.

But the majority of US/UK spelling differences are not of the *pajamas/pyjamas* type. Splits along the line of *color/colour* and *organize/organise* go through whole chunks of vocabulary, and they didn't come about from unfamiliarity with new borrowed words; they came about from intentional decisions to be different.

It started with dictionaries. When the pilgrims set sail for the colonies, English dictionaries didn't exist yet, so there were none to bring. They did have books though, and that's what determined the spelling conventions of the day. But different publishers used different spellings, not even all that consistently, and there was no one generally accepted standard. Words were spelled in many ways.

The first English dictionary of major authority was Samuel Johnson's *A Dictionary of the English Language*, published in London in 1755. It played an important role in establishing a spelling standard for English. Though many writers of the time did use the *-or* form in words like *honor*, *favor*, and *color*, Johnson opted for the *-our* versions.

But a few decades later America had become its own nation, and an educator named Noah Webster thought that a new nation deserved a new, more sensible spelling system. He thought America "should be as independent in literature as she is in politics." Why keep unreasonable spellings just because they were handed down that way from the Old World?

He proposed various spelling reforms, eliminating silent letters all over the place and making adjustments that he thought showed how a reasonable person would spell. He thought *machine, guillotine, soup, daughter, give,* and *believe* could just as well be *masheen, gillotin, soop, dawter, giv,* and *beleev.* Most of these ideas were ridiculed and failed to catch on.

But some did catch on, and they eventually came to represent the American way of spelling. The first version of his American dictionary was published in 1806. He tossed the *u* out of words like *honor, favor,* and *color.* He replaced *centre* with *center, defence* with *defense, plough* with *plow, draught* with *draft,* and *gaol* with *jail.*

Back in England, they went along with the idea of dropping the *k* from words like *magick*, since even at the time of Johnson's dictionary those spellings were looking old-fashioned. But they began to label other Webster spellings as *Americanisms* and regarded them with disdain. That disdain probably helped solidify habits like the *ou* in *colour* and the *re* in *centre* as British, even though they had been flexible on those spellings before *color* and *center* came to be seen as American.

A tendency developed, which the linguist Lynne Murphy has termed "orthographic patriotism," to choose particular spellings because Americans do it the other way, or because of the impression that it is typically American to do it the other way. The *-ize* ending, for example, came to be seen as American rather recently. It was a well-established part of English, and while Johnson's dictionary didn't include many *-ize/-ise* words, it did have *egotize, gourmandize, mythologize, mysterize,* and *tantalize,* alongside *tyrannise* and *synonomise.*

Webster mostly went with *-ize,* but it didn't take everywhere it might have. Americans still use *advertise, improvise, compromise,* and *televise.* Spelling remained variable in Britain. When the next great British dictionary, the *Oxford English Dictionary,* was published near the end of the nineteenth century, the editors gave prominence to the *-ize* option, on etymological grounds (the ending traces back to the Greek letter zeta).

It wasn't until the 1990s that *-ize* dramatically fell out of favor in Britain. With the rise of the internet and the opportunity to see more of other countries' spelling habits, *-ize* versus *-ise* became a self-fulfilling mark of national differentiation. The *z* spelling was more common with Americans, so it came to be seen as a mark of Americanness. In response, the *s* spelling came to be seen as a mark of Britishness.

There are a number of other patterns characteristic of a US/UK spelling split, such as *traveled/travelled, pediatric/paediatric, analyze/analyse,* and *tire/tyre.* And there is a common assumption that the US spelling is always the newer innovation. Depending on where you're from, you consider it either the fresher and more economical version or the corrupted and vulgar version. But actually it's rarely the case that the US version was an innovation at all.

The spellings that Webster promoted only worked when they were already an option. *Color* and *vigor* and *neighbor* and *organize* all had been used with those spellings long before the United States existed. Their *-our* and *-ise* spellings became identified with the United Kingdom not because they were older or more traditional but simply because the United States had claimed the other option. Different nations who speak the same language sometimes do things to add their own flavor. Or flavour.

Blame Ourselves

As we have seen, there is plenty of blame to go around for the messed up, illogical situation English finds itself in. The barbarians gave us old patterns and word-formation habits that became so entrenched that the updates passed them over when the world changed around them. The French came in, dismantled the writing system, and flooded all kinds of areas with their own vocabulary and phrasing, which persisted long after they themselves switched over to English. The printing press spread certain spelling habits, and they got so firmly rooted that it was too hard to change them when the pronunciation habits changed. The snobs made decisions about correctness based on personal taste and got us to go along with them by making us feel insecure.

Over the centuries, as English became increasingly written, taught, codified, standardized, and used in official institutions, not only did the language change, but our idea of what the language *is* changed. In the Middle Ages people thought Latin was a real language, a perfected language, a language of rules, while English was just . . . something people did. Now we think of English as a real language. We expect it to follow rules and conform to logic. But we forget that it is also still just something people do.

This was true of Latin too, though that was hard to see in the Middle Ages, because while Latin then was the language of scholarly, administrative, and religious realms, it wasn't used for regular life. There weren't Latin conversations about changing diapers, fixing door hinges, or peeling potatoes. It was no longer just something people did.

But at one time it had been, and when it was, there was just as much complaining about how it was changing and how sloppy, ignorant people were ruining it. In the third, fourth, or fifth century (dating is uncertain) a fed-up grammarian wrote up a list of Latin mistakes that were getting on his nerves.

It's *Februarius*, not *Febrarius*, he complained. *Auris*, not *oricla*; *calida*, not *calda*; *tabula*, not *tabla*. People were dropping syllables, switching up vowels, messing up the system. The grammarian's complaints failed to stop the deviance. Latin speakers kept on with their bad habits until those bad habits gave rise to new languages in which they were considered good habits.

The second syllable of *Februarius* stayed lost as it turned into Italian *febbraio*, Spanish *febrero*, and French *février*. The mispronunciation of the diphthong *au* vowel of *auris* (ear) as an *o* in *oricla* resulted in Italian *orecchia*, Spanish *oreja*, and French *oreille*. When *calida* (hot) lost a syllable as it was lazily pronounced *calda*, the shortened version lived on to be Italian *calda*, and eventually, through French, English *scald*. Similarly, the "lazy" version of *tabula* lived on as Spanish *tabla* and eventually (again through French) as English *table*. One era's annoying mistake is a future era's unimpeachable standard.

All languages have rules—even unwritten, uncodified vernaculars. Linguistic rules are patterns, conventions for making utterances that conform to certain general (though much debated) principles of human language ability.

Languages that are written, codified, and standardized also have explicitly endorsed or prescribed rules. Rules that are taught and enforced to a certain degree, but not necessarily followed. Correctness in language can be defined in relation to rules that are either tacit conventions or explicitly formalized prescriptions. Over time, because language is something people do, both kinds of rules will change.

Language also interacts with formal logic, the axioms and rules of inference, but it plays by its own rules. Human language utterances can mean things in a way that logic equations don't. Logically, "P and Q" should be the same as "Q and P," but *by and large* means something in a way that *large and by* does not. Because we write language out in a straight line of individual words, we tend to view the words as independent actors, each contributing a little piece of meaning to the whole in a predictable, rule-bound way. But language is not so orderly. The pieces don't add up.

The weirdness of English can be blamed on its history. Barbarians, French conquerors, printing, and snobs have all played their role. But we also have to blame ourselves. Language is a habit. We learn to do it from how the people around us do it. But we can do things with it that we have never heard anyone else do, create sentences that never existed before, make new meanings out of old expressions. When it comes to language, we are creatures of habit and creatures of creativity. It seems those two forces would pull us in opposite directions, but we manage to have it all at once.

"Blame ourselves" is not something that happens, in historical order, after all the other blames have been assigned. It has been there the whole time. And it's not unique to English. All languages are at the mercy of these opposing forces and find ways to resolve the contradictions.

But we are here to talk about English. Admittedly, this final section is kind of a grab bag, a place to put the answers for all the things I couldn't blame on the other groups. These questions have explanations that are related to history, but also to the way we humans mold language—not as something we control but as something that we do.

We hold on to some habits and discard others without worrying about whether the result makes sense ("Couth, Kempt, and Ruthful"; "If It Ain't Broke, Don't Scramble It"; "Proving the Rule"; "Abbreviation Deflation"; "Release the Meese"). We let words change their categories ("How Dare You Say 'How Try You!'") and expand in many meaning directions ("Why Do Noses Run and Feet Smell?"). At the same time we keep strict but hidden limits on them ("Negative Fixation"). Some things we just do, and it's hard to say why ("How It Comes to Be"; "Phrasal Verbs—Let's Go Over Them").

A jumble of influences have given us a vast array of resources we can exploit when we want to describe the weirdness of English. It's because of the barbarians we can call it *weird*. Also *odd, mad,* or *untidy*. Because of the French we can call it *strange, irregular,* or *disorganized*. Thanks to the snobs, we can say it's *anarchic, peculiar,* or even *sui generis*.

But we also have the means to create new resources out of old materials and constantly alter what we already have in order to keep things exciting ("Terrible and Terrific, Awful and Awesome";

"Literally Messed Up"). Thanks to this creative power we can also call English *scary ridonkulous* and *literally bananas*. We can blame ourselves for exploiting this creative power along with our historical inheritance, but we really wouldn't want it any other way. We get the blame, but we also get the benefit.

Couth, Kempt, and Ruthful

Why Have Some Words Lost Their Better Halves?

Some words seem to only have a grumpy, negative version. A person can be uncouth, unkempt and ruthless, but why can't they be the opposite?

In fact, at one time they could be. Some of these unpaired negative words were formed on the Old English layer of the language, when *couth* meant "known," as well as "familiar," "pleasant," or "cozy." It's related to *kith*, as in *kith and kin*: the people you know and the people you're related to. So *uncouth* was "alien, unfamiliar, strange," and eventually today's "uncultured and bad mannered." *Kempt* was how you said "combed" in Old English (when the verb "to comb" was *kemb*), and *ruth* was the "quality of rueing"—feeling compassion or pity—in the way that *growth* was the "quality of growing." A compassionate, merciful person was *ruthful*.

Other words formed on this old Germanic layer are *hapless*, *unwieldy*, and *ungainly*. *Hap* meant "luck" or "fortune." *Hapless* was "unlucky" before it came to mean "incompetent." There was no contrasting *hapful*, but there was *happy*—which originally meant "fortunate." To be *wieldy* meant "to be capable of easily wielding your limbs or your weapons." Light, quick, and agile. *Gain* meant "straight" or "direct," as in "the gainest road." Something *gainly* is direct, useful, and helpful. *Ungainly* is unpleasant, incompetent, and awkward.

The streak of partnerless negatives doesn't end with the old layer. The next layer, when French and Latin flooded in, contributed an enormous number of these words. *Indelible, incorrigible, disconsolate, impeccable, ineffable, inscrutable, incessant, indefatigable*; these all first came in their negative forms in the fifteenth and sixteenth centuries. While there were some later forms like *delible* (deletable), *corrigible* (correctible), *consolate* (comforted), and *peccable* (liable to sin), they quickly fell out of use, except in cases where they were used extremely self-consciously for showy or humorous effect. In the seventeenth century we do find *effable* (speakable), *scrutable* (understandable by scrutiny), *cessant* (ceasing), and *defatigable* (easily fatigued), but no evidence that they were in regular circulation.

In a few cases, the un-negated root word had been brought into the language much earlier. We had *appoint* before *disappoint* and *mantle* long before *dismantle*, but we would no longer consider those words to be opposites. *Disappoint* does not mean "undo an appointment" (although it used to), and *dismantle* means "to take apart," while the verb *mantle* meant "to cover or put a cloak on."

Disgruntled is the word that probably inspires the most humorous play, because it's just so much fun to say *gruntled*. In this case, the root word predates the *dis-* version by more than two hundred years. To *gruntle* meant making little grunty complaining sounds all the time, which is not really the positive counterpart to the grumpy *disgruntled*. That's because *dis-* here is not an opposite maker but an intensifier. It's the same one used in *disturb*, where *turba* is Latin for "turmoil."

So we might have just gone and formed the word *gruntled* for this meaning if we wanted, but why complain only a little when you can do it intensified?

Why does it seem like so many words for negative characteristics or states have lost their positive counterparts? Is that really even the case? Are there also positive words that have lost their negative counterparts? We certainly don't seem to notice as much the gaps in our vocabulary where there should, by similar logic of word analysis, be a negative counterpart for a positive word. We joke about the missing flipsides of *hapless*, *ruthless*, and *feckless*, but not what we should be able to form but don't from *bashful*, *grateful*, and *wistful*. There aren't many jokes about the *bashless*, *grateless*, and *wistless*.

The main reason more negatives have lost their positive partners is that we have prefixes and suffixes that form a negative of a word but none that do the reverse. We can make a clean thing sound dirty by calling it *unclean*, but we can't make a dirty thing sound clean by making it *undirty*. *Unhappy* makes sense, but *unsad* sounds wrong, and not very positive at all. Attaching *-ful* to a word doesn't make it positive, just full of the thing it attaches to (*hateful, shameful, harmful*).

If a prefixed or suffixed word becomes frequent enough, it may develop an independent identity, no longer seeming composed of two parts at all. This happened, for example, to *atone* and *alone*, which started as *at one* and *all one*. Then, language change can affect the root without affecting the affixed word. The pronunciation of *one*, formerly closer to 'own,' changed to 'wun,' but not in *atone* and *alone*. Similarly, *kempt* changed to *combed*, but not in *unkempt*. If one day the language has changed to the point where *clean* has become *cayn* and *dirty* has become *dorgy*, we might still be left with an unpartnered *unclean* to joke about, but we won't have an *undirty* with which to do the same.

When words don't have a positive partner, it's usually because a negative prefix once attached itself to another word that then became obsolete. At least these words get to live on in some way, negative though it may be.

If It Ain't Broke, Don't Scramble It

Why Is There No Egg in Eggplant?

Languages develop inconsistencies because language changes, but they develop just as many because language stays the same. This is why there is no egg in eggplant. Because eggplants changed, but the word for them didn't.

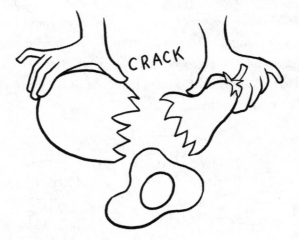

Originally, the word *eggplant* made perfect sense. It was first used in the eighteenth century to describe the small, white variety of the fruit. The name couldn't have been simpler or more straightforward: a plant growing this variety looks like it is bearing eggs. What's the most boring, basic thing you could call a plant that grows "eggs" on it? An egg plant, of course.

Eggplants were around long before they made their way to England, in many different varieties with many different names, throughout Asia and the Middle East. They were cooked in many different styles, and English travelers had encountered them and sometimes even enjoyed eating them. But the fruit known as *bandanjan* in Hindi, *patlijan* in Turkish, and *qiézi* in Mandarin was not embraced as food at first, but as a garden ornament.

As eggplants became more widely known in Europe during the Renaissance, they were given the Latin name *mala insana*, or "insane apple." Like other so-called nightshade plants, it had a bad reputation and was considered at worst poisonous and at best liable to put you in a bad mood (on account of its bitterness). But they grew so well in warm southern Europe that people began to eat more and more of them, and ultimately to love them quite a bit. *Mala insana* is the source of the Italian word for eggplant, *melanzana*.

In England, it took a longer time for the eggplant to be viewed as food. In 1597 the English botanist John Gerard acknowledged that people do eat it in other places without ill effects but added, "I rather wishe Englishmen to content themselves with the meate and sauce of our own country than with the fruite and sauce eaten with such peril: for doubtlesse these apples have a mischievous property; the use thereof is to be utterly forsaken." He had to admit they were pretty cool-looking, though, which is why he advised, "It is better to esteem this plant and have him in the garden for your pleasure and the rarenesse thereof, then for any virtue or good qualities yet knowne."

So the *mala insana* made its way into English-speaking territory as a garden decoration. The first citation for the word *eggplant* is from a 1767 guide titled *Every Man His Own Gardener*, where it is grouped with some pretty flowers: "The choicest kinds [of tender annuals] are the double balsams . . . ice plant, egg plant and China aster."

Eventually, the English-speaking world discovered the less bitter, more delicious "purple-fruited eggplant." The nearby French were introducing them to exotic, savory dishes made with what they called *aubergine*. As people in England became more familiar with the possibilities of eggplant in the dining room, they also imported this foodier word for it.

But this was already near the turn of the twentieth century, when it was too late for the United States. Eggplant was called *eggplant*, and when it changed from something you looked at to something you ate, the name had already lost any obvious connection to its literal-description roots. Eggplants were just eggplants whatever their color, and while the word stayed, the perfectly reasonable justification for the name was lost. Language drifts and changes, but it also very much prefers to leave well enough alone as much as possible.

Proving the Rule

How Can an Exception Prove a Rule?

An exception to a rule is a counterexample, and usually a counterexample is proof that a rule is not a rule at all. If I aim to prove that teenagers are incapable by nature of cleaning their rooms and I find one who loves to clean his room and does it diligently every day, my case is not helped at all but damaged. The exception is evidence against my rule.

Still, it wouldn't be unusual to say about such a teenager, "He's the exception that proves the rule!"

When the phrase is used this way, it's a form of saying, "Look, here's something noteworthy!" It says that there's a general rule: that teenagers don't clean their rooms—and an exception that doesn't fit: the kid who loves to clean his room. But it doesn't say anything about one proving the other. How did this idiom come to be?

The exception proves the rule is based on the Latin phrase *exceptio probat regulam*, a legal principle that can be used to argue the following: if exceptions are made under specific conditions, it must mean there is a rule that applies when those conditions are not in effect. If a sign on a concrete plaza at a school says the following:

"No Skateboarding When School Is in Session," you can infer that you are allowed to skateboard at other times. The rule that the exception proves is that skateboarding is generally allowed. If that were not the rule, why would exceptions be made at all? Why not just say "No Skateboarding?"

The fuller version of the Latin maxim is *exceptio probat regulam in casibus non exceptis*. This makes the meaning more explicit: exception proves the rule in cases where the exception doesn't apply. It can also appear with *firmat/confirmat/figit* instead of *probat* (exception *establishes/confirms/fixes* the rule).

When the phrase drifted from its original, legalistic meaning sometime in the seventeenth century, it was probably helped along by its similarity to sayings like "There's an exception to every rule." It was also influenced by a different sense of *rule*, not the legal sense of a standard of what is allowed or prohibited but a looser sense, meaning the normal or usual state of things.

This is the sense we use when we say things like "As a rule, I bring my lunch from home." This isn't a declaration that I have a strict policy about never buying lunch at work. It's just saying what I ordinarily do. Something that happens "as a rule" is assumed to have occasional exceptions.

So "as a rule" teenagers don't clean their rooms. It's the usual state of affairs, the generalization, the stereotype. The kid who loves to clean his room is unusual, an outlier. But to be an outlier, he has to be an outlier to something. A general tendency, a rule. He proves the rule by being surprising.

This may not be what people have in mind every time they use the phrase, but there is a pathway in the language over time from legal maxim to comment about unusual states of affairs. It involves different ideas of what is a rule, a principle, an axiom, a regulation, versus the typical, the expected, the norm. There was a ready-made phrase, already in use for the first sense, that we co-opted for the second sense.

How Dare You Say "How Try You"!

Why *Dare* Isn't Like the Other Verbs

There's something very weird about *dare*. It's not like other verbs. It dares to be different.

"How *dare* you say that!" is a normal English sentence, but that kind of sentence structure doesn't work with many verbs. "How *try* you say that"? "How *know* you say that"? "How *prefer* you say that"? Not normal at all.

There is a limited set of verbs that do work in that structure though. "How *can/could/must/will/should* you say that" are all fine options. That limited set of verbs belongs to a class called modals, auxiliaries, or sometimes "helping" verbs. They express things like likelihood, possibility, ability, obligation, and permission.

There are various ways in which modals don't behave like other verbs. For example, they don't take the -*s* ending in the third person (He cans play Hamlet), and they don't have an infinitive form with *to* (To should be, or not to should be). They also aren't followed by infinitive forms (I must to be, or I must not to be).

Dare acts like a modal verb in *how dare you*, but it can also do things modal verbs don't do. *Dare* can *dare to be different*, but *can* can't *can to be different* and *should* shouldn't *should to be different*. Full verbs, outside of the set of modals, are fine here. *Try* can *try to be different*, *know* can *know to be different*, and *prefer* can *prefer to be different*.

The older uses of *dare* are in the modal camp, but *dare* drifted away from this group in the sixteenth century and became more like other verbs. It is now used as a main verb with all the forms main verbs can take (e.g., *to dare, dares, dared, daring*). But it still has a foot in the modal group, trying to have it both ways, making it act a little weird sometimes.

The modal uses of *dare* now sound a bit old-fashioned. Phrases like "They dare not go," "Dare I look?" or "I dare say" belong to another era, while "Dare to be different" is thoroughly modern.

Dare isn't the only one that can be main or modal. Another English verb with one foot in the regular and one foot in the modal category is *need*. Unlike *dare*, though, *need* started as a regular verb. It drifted over to the modal group starting in the sixteenth century. Modal *need* made sentences like "Need he complain so much?" and "He needn't make so many demands" possible. This phrasing sounds old-fashioned now, but there was a time when it was new.

Both modal *dare* and modal *need* never fully joined the *can/could/must/will/should* club. They are more restricted in how they can be used, mainly in questions and sentences with some kind of negative force, licensed by words like *not, only, hardly*, and *seldom* (see "Negative Fixation"). They are also going out of style, sounding more quaint as the years go by.

The modal *dare* of *how dare you* survives as a useful hand-me-down, a relic from an earlier time. It remains a deliciously dramatic way to express indignation. I daresay it needn't ever be retired.

Release the Meese

Why Isn't the Plural of *Moose Meese*?

A moose is a moose, but what if there are two?

Even though we've got juices, truces, uses, deuces, and cabooses, we don't have mooses. We just have moose, whether it's two moose or a hundred and two. But there is a temptation to treat it like a different kind of animal with a similar name, the goose, and say *two meese*. Why isn't that how it ended up?

The plural of *goose* has been *geese* since the earliest days of English. This type of irregular noun, where the plural is marked by a change in the vowel, comes from a process in the Germanic ancestor of English. There was a plural ending *-i*, which was a vowel made with the tongue body toward the front of the mouth (an 'ee' sound). When it was added to a noun root like *fot* (foot), it pulled the vowel of the root forward. (The process is known as "umlaut.") Eventually *fot-foti* and *toth-tothi* became *foot-feet* and *tooth-teeth*.

The *-i* ending was no longer needed. The root vowel showed whether the word was plural.

There are a few other irregular plurals in English that are the result of umlaut: *lice, mice, men*, and, of course, *geese*. *Moose* wasn't even a gleam in the eye of English vocabulary when these were formed. It was borrowed more than a thousand years later, in the seventeenth century, from the Algonquian native languages explorers encountered in what would come to be New England.

By then, there was only one productive way to form new plurals in English. Add an *s*. The *-s* ending had taken over the older Germanic patterns like umlaut (*boc-bec* became *book-books*) and *-er* and *-en* (both still survive in *children*, but *kine, eyen*, and *housen* were replaced by *cows, eyes*, and *houses*).

So, going by other words that were borrowed from Algonquian languages at this time, *moose* should have fallen in line with the general English plural rule, as did *persimmons, moccasins, raccoons, opossums*, and *skunks*.

Instead, *moose* went the way of a different plural form that had been in use since Old English: the plural that leaves the word just as it is, the zero plural. Nouns were classified then as masculine, feminine, or neuter, and a specific class of neuter nouns, including *deer, swine*, and *sheep*, had zero-marked plurals. Those words still have zero plurals, but there are other words that took on that plural strategy later. These words were either in Old English but not in the neuter class in Old English, like *fish*, which once had the plural *fiscas*, or they were borrowed from other languages like *salmon* and *quail* (from French) and *caribou* and *moose* from Native American languages.

It's pretty unusual for an old, irregular pattern to pick up so many new converts. When an irregular pattern takes on a new life by extending itself to new territory, it's usually because of similar forms. For example, the verb *ring-ringed-ringed* was changed, by analogy, to *ring-rang-rung* because *ring* had such a sound similarity to *sing*. In contrast, the words that took on zero plurals had no sound similarity to the original zero plurals at all.

But they did have meaning similarity. The animals that zero plural holds for now stand in a particular kind of relationship to humans: one where the humans hunt or catch the animals for food. *Moose, elk, antelope, caribou, bison, buffalo, fish, salmon, cod, grouse*—all can be found in the bare plural form, and others that usually take a regular plural, such as *squirrels* and *crabs*, can have zero plural forms in some hunting contexts: "Those woods are full of squirrel." "Use deep water pots to catch crab."

ZERO PLURAL

MOOSE   DEER   BUFFALO

Old zero plurals like *sheep* and *swine* don't fit in this meaning relationship. Humans don't chase and hunt sheep or swine; they raise them, like they do cows, pigs, lambs, chickens, goats, and all kinds of animals that take a regular plural *-s*.

While *swine* has generally been replaced by the more common *pigs* or *hogs*, *sheep* are still *sheep*, a surviving remnant of an old linguistic habit.

And *deer* are still *deer*, an animal which plays a huge role in the human hunting relationship and is likely the origin of its association with that meaning. *Deer* (*deor* in Old English) originally referred to any kind of four-legged land animal. (It traces back to the same source as the modern German word *Tier*, which still has that more general meaning.) Over time, as deer hunting became a culturally important activity in England, with elaborate rituals and vast tracts of land set aside by the aristocracy just for its practice, *deer* came to mean not just any animal but the deer of the hunt.

The zero plural then became a habit for fish and game birds, but *geese*, with its own very old, entrenched habit, resisted the trend. When English speakers encountered the moose in the New World, they heard a word that that sounded like *goose* but saw an animal that looked like an extra-large deer, and they treated it like one, both in how they hunted it and how they talked about it.

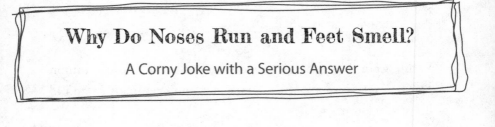

Why Do Noses Run and Feet Smell?

A Corny Joke with a Serious Answer

SNIFF SNIFF

At first glance this whole topic seems like just an old groaner of a joke:

> *If your nose is running and your feet smell . . . you must be upside down!*

But there is a little more to it than it might seem. Even in a joke this tired and corny there are some interesting linguistic facts to discover.

You start to see what's interesting about it when you compare it with the way other old groaners and puns work.

> *Why was 6 afraid of 7? Because 7 8 9!*

Here we have a joke based on the fact that two completely different, unrelated words, the one for the number eight and the one for the past tense of the verb *to eat*, happen to be pronounced the same way. *Eight* and *ate* are what we call homophones (from Greek roots for "same" + "sounds"), and the joke is based on that.

What has four wheels and flies? A garbage truck.

In this case the ambiguity that makes the joke is a little different, as both senses of *fly*, the verb for moving through the air and the noun for the insect, are indeed related. A fly is something that flies. They are what we call polysemous (from Greek roots for "many" + "meanings"). This joke wouldn't have worked in Old English, because there were different endings for verbs and nouns. (It either has four wheels and *fliegth* or four wheels and *fleogan*.) But word endings that showed the roles of nouns and verbs gradually disappeared or were greatly reduced in English, leaving just *-s* as the marker for third person singular verb—and in a set of other, unrelated developments, also as the marker for plural nouns.

What did the mayonnaise say when the refrigerator door opened?
"Close the door! I'm dressing!"

Again we have historical polysemy. Meanings that are different but related. *To dress* was borrowed from French and meant to set up or prepare. In English it came to primarily mean "to put clothes on" (a type of setting up or preparing), while the noun *dressing* came to primarily mean a sauce to put on salad (from a type of setting up or preparing you do with food). The ambiguity here comes from the fact that the -*ing* can be a verb ending or a noun ending.

So what about noses running and feet smelling? In these cases, there's no ambiguity having to do with word endings and parts of speech. *Run* and *smell* are verbs whether the subjects are track stars and sommeliers or noses and feet. And the different meanings of *run* and *smell* that drive the joke do not mean that they have homophones. This is not a "seven ate nine" situation.

Both *run* and *smell* are polysemous, though. They have constellations of different but related meanings, especially so in the case of *run*, which has the most definitions of any word in the *Oxford English Dictionary*. You can run errands, run away, run for office, run aground, run on caffeine, run a company, run into an old friend. Colors run, engines run, Broadway shows run. The dictionary entry for *run* runs on and on.

RUN   RUN   RUN   RUN

But the most basic, primary definition for *run* is, as the dictionary puts it, "to go with quick steps on alternate feet." The definition related to the flow of liquid is also very old and basic. People and horses ran and blood and water ran from the earliest days of English. They are united by a core sense of fast motion from one place to another.

The ambiguity of running noses doesn't just come from the two competing meanings of "going fast on legs" and "flowing liquid." There is another layer on top of the competing meanings. When liquids "run," the liquid is usually the subject. Lava runs down the mountain. Syrup runs off the edge of the plate. Tears run. Rivers run.

But when it comes to noses, it's not the liquid that's the subject but the place where the liquid is coming from. The snot runs, yes, but so does the nose. This is an unusual twist. There are just a few other things that can be the subject in this way: sores, eyes, faucets, and taps. To switch between the two interpretations of running noses, we have to switch between a nose with a very passive role (just sitting there emitting snot) and a very active one (moving those little feet).

A similar switch takes place with the different interpretations of feet smelling. *Smell* is one of a special class of words known as verbs of perception. This class includes words having to do with our senses like *taste*, *feel*, *hear*, *see*. Verbs of perception can have three different kinds of subjects: The active performer of the verb, the experiencer of the verb, or the percept subject, which is, basically, the thing that results in an experiencer having the experience of a perception.

Ugh, OK, sorry, that simple explanation got increasingly less simple there. Let's use a more concrete example. For the sense of sound, there are three different verbs for the three types: *listen*, *hear*, and *sound*:

Frank listened to the birds singing.

Frank actively does something to experience a perception.

Frank heard the birds singing.

Frank experiences a perception whether or not he actively does anything.

The birds sounded happy.

The birds create a perception available to Frank.

The ambiguity comes in for perception verbs that use the same form for all three types, and *smell* is one of those.
Active: *Frank stopped and smelled the doughnuts.*
Experiencer: *Frank smelled doughnuts as he passed by the bakery.*
Percept subject: *The doughnuts smelled delicious.*

SMELL   SMELL   SMELL

English is not unusual in the way it uses the same words for different types of perception verbs, but other languages may carve out the types differently. In Italian you wouldn't use the verb for smell, *sentire*, for the percept subject: doughnuts can't "smell delicious," but they can "have a delicious scent." In German there is a verb *düften* that specifically means "to smell good," but you can only use it for the percept subject (the flowers *düften*). However, in Danish the related verb *dufte* can be used as an experiencer type. (I *dufte* that wonderful dinner you are cooking.)

English doesn't have a verb that means "to smell good," but it has some that mean "to smell bad" (and can only be used for percept subject), like *stink* and *reek*. *Smell* itself also means smell bad when it occurs without any descriptor after it. I can tell you your feet smell good or your feet smell bad, but if I just say "Your feet smell," it only means the latter.

The weirdness of noses running and feet smelling doesn't implicate English specifically but language in general. It's a consequence of the complicated way humans layer grammatical roles (subject, object), semantic roles (what is acting, what is experiencing, what is emitting), and meaning (running with feet or flowing? Good smell or bad smell?).

There are many places in language where there are conflicting readings of the relation between grammar roles, semantic roles, and meaning. In daily life, where context resolves those conflicts for us, they slip by unnoticed. But when they do get noticed, they might end up in an academic article, a philosophy paper, or a simple corny joke.

Negative Fixation

Why Can You Say "This Won't Take Long" but Not "This Will Take Long"?

Most sentences in English, or any other language, can be negative or affirmative.

> I don't like pears.
> I like pears.

> We don't have news for you.
> We have news for you.

> This won't take all day.
> This will take all day.

So why is it that "This won't take long" sounds so wrong in the affirmative? Why can't we say "This will take long?"

Sure, "This will take a long time" or "This will take longer than usual" works just fine. There's no problem expressing the meaning of "This will take long"; we just can't use that form to do it.

Take long belongs to the special and somewhat mysterious class of expressions that linguists call negative polarity items. These items can't occur in simple affirmative statements. There are different types of negative polarity items. They can be pronouns or particles like *any, yet, either,* or *at all;* nouns like *a thing, an iota, a drop, a crap, a peep, a red cent;* verbs like *budge;* or phrases like *breathe a word, hold a candle, have a clue, sleep a wink, lift a finger.* They can only occur in a negative sentence frame:

> *There aren't any here* vs. *There are any here*
> *He didn't have a red cent to his name* vs. *He had a red cent to his name*
> *The boulder won't budge* vs. *The boulder will budge*
> *I don't think we will sleep a wink* vs. *I think we will sleep a wink*

Actually, though, that's not quite the whole story. They are called negative polarity items because they are most allowable in negative frames, but they can also be in questions (*Do you see any?*), if-clauses (*If you make a peep, you'll get in trouble*), and contexts with words like *without, doubt, surprise,* and *regret* (*I regret lifting a finger to help*). The conditions for what works for which items are not all the same, and there are different theories for the reasons behind those conditions, having to do with meaning, attitude, implication, and logic. It's complicated!

Take long is a negative polarity item. It can't be in a straight-forward affirmative statement like "This will take long." But these kinds of items don't just drop out of nowhere with the negative-frame requirement already in place. *Long*, as an adverb meaning "a long time," had long been in use for positive contexts (like this one right here) before the first negative uses of "take long" showed up in the late seventeenth century.

There were uses that now sound archaic like "Though he held the treasure long" (from *Beowulf*) and those that sound a little formal like "We have long expected this," but there are still plenty of completely current uses like *before long* or *all day long*.

When *long* modified verbs to mean "for a long duration," it could be positive or negative. In "held the treasure long" or "have long expected," it is the verb, the holding or the expecting, that has a long duration. But in the seventeenth century it began to be used with a slightly different meaning, as a substitute for the noun phrase "a long time" with verbs like *need, require, spend,* and *take*. In "They didn't need/require/spend/take long," it is not that the duration of the needing, requiring, spending, or taking had (or rather didn't have) a long duration. It is that the object of the verb, a long stretch of time, was not needed, required, spent, or taken.

The difference is subtle, and it is not clear why this use came about and why only in the negative frame. But the other use of *long*, the verb-duration-modifying one, started to behave more like a negative polarity item too. Whereas you could say "This gowne hath lasted him longe" in 1530, now "didn't last him long" is much better than "lasted him long." Likewise for other pairs where *long* can refer to the duration of the verb.

We didn't stay long vs. *We stayed long*
We didn't work long vs. *We worked long*

Expressions can become negative polarity items over time. *At all* used to mean "in every way, altogether," and in some dialects in Ireland and the United States it can still be used in an affirmative frame like "It's the greatest fun at all." But now it is overwhelmingly found in negative polarity frames like *none at all, can't at all, didn't at all*.

With some of the more idiomatic negative polarity expressions we have a very good idea of how they came to be negative. Some, like "lift a finger" go back to sayings that were negatives in their original sources. *Lift a finger* goes back to the Bible, Matthew 23:4: "They themselves will not move them with one of their fingers." Others like *hold a candle* first had a straightforward meaning— to hold a candle up for someone else so they could have light to work—and then acquired a metaphorical sense in the negative, that someone so deficient in comparison to a worthy person is not even fit to do the candle-holding job for them.

It's also possible for expressions to go the other way, to start as negative polarity items and become OK in affirmative contexts. In some dialects *anymore* is used to mean now or nowadays, such as in "Gas is expensive anymore." Other expressions have moved into affirmative frames but still retain negative implications.

You don't know diddly squat.

You know diddly squat.

(*Diddly squat* has itself become a negative word meaning "nothing.")

Do you mind the noise?

As a matter of fact, I mind it a lot.

(Affirmative *mind* implies an objection.)

There can be subtle movement and change with respect to how the parts of a language interact with negation, and there are no simple explanations for why negative polarity items act the way they do. It can be especially hard for nonnative speakers to learn the subtleties of usage.

But this is not something weird about English. The phenomenon of negative polarity items is found in a variety of human languages. Research in this area is still relatively new, but it appears to reveal something about language, and the intersection of language and logic, in general. We can blame this weirdness on ourselves. One day we should know more, but it might take long.

Abbreviation Deflation

Why Is There an *R* in *Mrs.*?

English has a number of written abbreviations for the titles we use to address people, and they are pretty straightforward. We just pronounce them as if they were fully written out. *Mr.* is read as "mister," *Dr.* as "doctor," *Prof.* as "professor," *Rev.* as "reverend," *Jr.* as "junior," and *Esq.* as "esquire." But something strange happens for *Mrs.* If we write *Mrs.* and say "missus," why is there an *r* in there at all?

The simple answer is that *Mrs.* is an abbreviation for *mistress*. Except it isn't, really. When it comes to English, even the simple answers are never quite simple. When we see the written text *Mrs.*, we do not read it out as "mistress" but as "missus." What's more, the meaning of the written abbreviated form is completely different from the meaning of *mistress*. *Mrs.* is the formal term of address for a married woman. A *mistress* is a paramour, a lover, someone you are not married to—in other words, the person you cheat on your *Mrs.* with.

The fully written-out word *mistress* has had many uses in English since it was first borrowed from the French *maîtresse* (*maistresse* in the older version of French from which it was borrowed). A mistress could be a woman with some kind of authority over a household or commercial establishment, or authority over others such as children or servants. We still use it this way in *headmistress* or *mistress of ceremonies*.

In the seventeenth century it also came to refer to the "other woman" in an illicit relationship, probably through the idea not of authority but of notoriety. A similar thing happened with another title word we borrowed from French: *madam*. First it was a title for a grand lady of some position or authority, and then a kept woman, and eventually the woman in charge of a brothel.

In the case of both *mistress* and *madam*, a different, more relaxed pronunciation took over in certain situations: "missus" and "ma'am," which became so common and noticeable that they became their own, identifiable words. *Missus* and *ma'am* took on their own meanings and associations. Something similar happened with the titles *sir* and *mister*, which were at first slightly different pronunciations of *sire* and *master* and then totally different words of their own.

It is possible to both write and pronounce *ma'am*, *Sir*, and *Mr.* without ever knowing their connection to *madam*, *sire*, and *master*. It is also possible to write and pronounce *Mrs.* without ever knowing it had any connection to the word *mistress*. In fact, that is what the majority of us do, completely overlooking that there is a letter in there that has no business in an abbreviation of *missus*.

But *Mrs.* is not an abbreviation of the written word *missus*, which we hardly ever write out that way. It's a word. Spelled with a silent *r*, and pronounced as "missus," in the same way that *lbs.* is pronounced as "pounds." *Lbs.* is another example of something that started as an abbreviation, for Latin *libra pondo*, meaning a pound of weight as measured by a *libra*, or scale. But you don't have to know any of that to use *lbs.* in English, and you don't need to know that a *Mrs.* was once a *mistress*.

However, if you suddenly notice the absurdity and find yourself asking why, the answer, as usual, is there in the history.

How It Comes to Be

How Come We Say *How Come?*

At first glance, *how come* seems like just another way to say *why*. Indeed, there are many situations where it can substitute for *why*. If your roommate brings home a tank full of snakes, you can ask "How come?" And at the end of telling a story you can say, "And that's how come I'll never have another roommate."

How come definitely has a more casual feel than *why*, but if you look a little more closely, there are other ways in which it is not the same as *why* at all. For example, for *why* you need to make some changes to the sentence you're asking about. For the proposition "You are getting another dog" you have to switch the position of *you* and *are* to get "Why *are you* getting another dog?" If there's no helping verb already, you have to add a *do/does* before the subject, so "*You have* so many dogs" becomes "Why *do you have* so many dogs?" You have to do this for all the other question words as well (What do you feed them? Where do they sleep? How does your cat feel about this?).

How come doesn't act like a question word in this way. No verbs are switched, no *do* support added. When you ask a question with *how come*, the sentence is left just as it would be if it weren't in a question at all. How come [you are getting another dog]? How come [you have so many dogs]? How come [you are doing this to your cat]? *How come* might mean the same thing *why* does, but a sentence with *how come* is structured very differently from a *why* (or *who, what, where, when, how*) question.

How come acts like a phrase that introduces another clause with a *that* conjunction.

> Why is it that [you are getting another dog]?
> What is the reason that [you have so many dogs]?

In questions like these, the sentence that is expressing the thing you are asking about stays as is, without verb switching or *do* support.

But there is no *that* with *how come*. It seems to be a shortening of the longer phrase *how does it come to be that* [you are doing this to your cat]?

> How ~~does it~~ come ~~to be that~~ [you are doing this to your cat]?

It's possible that *how come* got shortened from that longer phrase, but not very likely. The earliest uses we have evidence for are in contexts like novels where the characters are using nonstandard, "uneducated" speech. And *how does it come to be that* is a pretty complex and formal place for colloquial *how come* to start. It's also infrequent in the texts of the previous centuries. Major shortenings tend to happen to very frequently used phrases, like *God be with you* (which became *goodbye*) or *how do you do* (which became *howdy*).

Far more frequent than the mouthful *how does it come to be that* in the centuries leading up to *how come* was a different type of question structure, one where you could just reverse the subject and verb, no *do* or other supporting verb necessary, as in *Where go they? What say you? How knows he this?*

It was possible to say things like these examples from Shakespeare:

How comes it, that thou are thus estranged from thyself?
How comes it that you have help to make this rescue?
How comes it that the subtle queen of Goths / is of a sudden
 thus advanced in Rome?

Phrases like these could possibly end up as *how come*, but they would have to shed a few important things to do so. The *that* could be left off easily, something we already do in many cases (compare *I wish that you would go / I wish you would go*). But the *it* and the *-s* ending on the verb *come* aren't as easily dispensed with. It would be as if we started saying *how goes it?* as *how go?*

How goes it has been around since the sixteenth century, and it has stayed frozen in that form ever since. *How comes it* isn't used at all anymore, having been replaced by *how does it come to be / come about / come to pass*, and also, in a way, by *how come*.

"In a way" because it's not completely clear that that's where it came from. For shortened expressions like *goodbye*, there is a record of in-between stages for the shortening. Forms like *god bwye*, *god b'uy*, and *good-b'wy* show up in various texts over the centuries of transition. There isn't a neat record of transition for *how comes it that* to *how come*, but there are related structures like "How came you to believe this?" and "How comes the change?" that may have had an influence on the development.

The earliest citations for *how come* appear in representations of the vernacular speech of African Americans, Native Americans, and German immigrants in the nineteenth century. This indicates that it began in nonstandard, non-written dialects. It may have also been used in nonstandard dialects of England. We don't see the modern use of *how come* until well into the twentieth century, but as the frequency of its use goes up beginning in the 1920s, the frequency of the "How came you to believe this" and "How comes it" types of uses falls off.

How come may have had humble origins, in a filtering of various types of phrases through nonnative understandings of English, but it proved so useful a pairing of form (a simple two syllables) and meaning (a complex "How does it come to be that") that it took over the standard.

Phrasal Verbs—Let's Go Over Them

But Don't Try to "Go Them Over" (You Can Look Them Over Though)

In the 1930s an eccentric British writer named C. K. Ogden put forward a new type of English language that he claimed would be easier to learn and simpler to use, and might even help people think more clearly. He called it Basic English, and it had a vocabulary of just 850 words. He claimed that those words should be enough to express almost anything normally expressed in English.

Why learn the word *disembark* when you could just as well say *get off a boat*? Why have *remove* when you could use *take away*? Ogden claimed that most verbs were unnecessary and pretty much any verbal idea could be expressed with a small number of "operators" like *come, go, get, put, take, have, give,* and *make*.

Basic English didn't get very far, but Ogden had noticed a neat feature of English that you could exploit if your goal was to cut down on words. Many verbs can indeed be replaced with multiword phrases. *Occur, happen, succeed, insult, tolerate,* and *surrender* can go if you've got *take place, come about, get ahead, put down, put up with,* and *give in.*

The problem is that reducing the vocabulary in this way wouldn't make English any easier to learn. These phrasal verbs (also called multipart verbs or particle verbs) are notoriously frustrating to people who have to learn English as a second language. Learners hate them almost as much as English spelling.

Even if you know the little words individually, you might not have any idea what they mean put together. *Look* and *up* are simple and clear. They make sense together in "Look up the hill." But you have to learn that they mean something different when put together in "Look up the address." Likewise, *look* and *after* are nice simple words in "You can look after twenty minutes." But they have fused together into a new type of word that must be learned on its own in "You can look after my pets." *Look up* has a meaning like *find. Look after* has a meaning like *supervise.*

There are a lot of phrasal verbs in English, and you have to learn them one by one, so you haven't saved much time by knowing the littler words that go into them. They may even make you waste more time by enticing you to puzzle out the reason they use the littler words they do. But memorizing a list of multi-word words isn't even the hard part. The hard part is learning how to put them into a sentence. Even though they act like one word with respect to meaning, the two parts can sometimes move around separately.

Look up the address is a good sentence. So is *look the address up* with the object inserted between the parts. *Look after my pets* is a good sentence. But *look my pets after* is not. No splitting up the parts on that one.

Why should that be? It is tempting to come up with an explanation based on meaning differences between "finding" and "supervising" or differences between the prepositions *up* and *after*, but such explanations are usually dead ends. If you come up with a reason based on meaning or preposition type, you end up with a long description that only works for one example and not as any kind of helpful rule. And then you have to start all over again when someone asks about *look over* and *go over*, which both mean "review" and both use the same preposition. If you have the report, you can *look it over*, but not *go it over*.

But can you *look over it*? Maybe? "I got the report; let's look over it" sounds fine to me, which is surprising, because usually if you substitute the object with a pronoun, you no longer simply *can* place it between the verb parts, you *must*. That seems to be a pretty general rule. You can tell someone to *look the address up* or *look it up*. You can't tell them to *look up it*. Nor can you *cheer up her*, or *figure out it*, or *tell off them*. In any case, those all sound a lot worse than *look over it*.

But maybe my instincts are starting to go haywire. That can happen after spending too long submerged in phrasal verbs searching for clarity. Is there clarity to be found?

Some of the challenges in learning to use phrasal verbs are not unique to English. All of the Germanic languages have some form of separable two-part verbs (in the Germanic linguistic literature they are called particle verbs instead of phrasal verbs). And they work differently in the different languages. Their meanings must also be memorized, and the principles that determine how they appear in sentences—together or separated, particle before or after the verb—are complicated and take time to master.

English phrasal verbs and the particle verbs of German, Dutch, Danish, Swedish, Norwegian, and Icelandic probably all developed from their shared Germanic origins, but it's difficult to pin down exactly how. Old English didn't have much in the way of these verbs. It did, however, have a lot of prefixed verbs. We still use some of them today, words like *understand* and *upbraid*.

Big changes to sentence structure happened between the arrival of the French in 1066 and the revival of writing in English two hundred years later. We don't have much of a written record of it, but we know that many prefixes and grammatical markers disappeared and word ordering for verbs and objects changed. When phrasal verbs like *give up* finally appear, they look less like the prefixed German- or Dutch-type verb (*aufgeben*, *opgeven*) and more like the Scandinavian, Danish, or Swedish type (*give op*, *ge upp*). The number of phrasal verbs slowly increased in the fourteenth and fifteenth centuries.

At the same time, French was working its way into the vocabulary with words that provided alternatives to the phrasal-verb creation strategy. *Give up* could also be *surrender* or *relinquish*. This probably slowed the proliferation of phrasal verbs for a while, but as English retook the written sphere, they came back strong and multiplied fast. Some of them were created as alternatives to Latin borrowings, which themselves came from prefix-verb constructions. For example, *eradicate* was first translated as *outroot* (its literal Latin meaning), which then became *root out*.

Phrasal verbs became extremely productive in English, especially in casual speech. Just as *find something out*, in the sense of getting to an answer, opened the way for *work it out*, *figure it out*, *make it out*, *puzzle it out*, and *suss it out*, *bug out* opened the way for *freak out*, *flip out*, and *wig out*. Once you could *gross someone out*, you could *creep them out*, *weird them out*, and even *squick them out*. Some of these formulations fall away, but even pretty slangy ones can eventually cross over to the standard language.

As these new verbs are formed, their grammatical habits, like whether they take an object or not (*clean up*, yes; *catch up*, no) are determined by the way people use them and can change. If you say "Catch me up on all the gossip," it might sound a bit slangy, but the meaning is clear. "Tell me all the gossip until I have caught up to your level of knowledge."

So what do you tell the poor English learner who wants to know what the rules are? That they simply have to learn a thousand phrasal verbs one by one? Luckily, while there isn't one nice set of rules to capture it all, or even twenty sets, there are clusters of types, such as the *work it out / figure it out / puzzle it out* type, that give you a pattern to work with that can lighten the load. After enough exposure, nonnative speakers of English get very good at phrasal verbs.

But no English speakers, native or not, get good at explaining why phrasal verbs act the way they do, no matter how much we break it down, lay it out, look it over, or go over it . . . we may not know exactly why we can't also "go it over," but we don't have to go it alone.

Terrible and Terrific, Awful and Awesome
How Does the Same Root Get Opposite Meanings?

The words *terrible* and *terrific* share something in common (dun dun DUNNNN *cue screaming*) . . . *terror*! So how did they get to be opposites?

They used to mean the same thing. They both were borrowed into English under the combined influence of French (*terrible*, *terrifique*) and Latin (*terribilis*, *terrificus*). *Terrible*, first attested around 1400, meant "fit to cause terror." *Terrific* came later, in the 1600s, and first had a similar meaning: something that is *terrific* causes terror. A monster, a storm, or a nightmare could be *terrible* or *terrific* in the sense that they brought on fear.

Today, both words have drifted away from the idea of terror. *Terrible* can just mean bad. A song, a movie, or a bowl of soup can be terrible without being scary at all. You can be a terrible piano player without causing any fear. In contrast, *terrific*, even though it also lost its association with fear, doesn't mean bad but the opposite. If you see a movie and you think it's terrible and your friend thinks it's terrific, you completely disagree.

You also disagree if you go out to dinner afterwards and you think the soup is awesome while your friend thinks it's awful. Both *awful* and *awesome* were formed on the word *awe*, which comes from an old Scandinavian word root for . . . terror.

Awe was originally a feeling of fear or dread, but the meaning developed into fear mixed with feelings of reverence. That development makes sense; you can fear someone because of their great authority or power and also respect their authority or power. From a type of religious, reverential fear, it developed into a sense of being humbled and impressed by what is before you. *Awful* was coined first, in the twelfth century, when the word *awe* still prominently predominantly implied fear. *Awesome* came much later, in the sixteenth century, when respect and wonder were more prominent.

As with *terrible*, *awful* mellowed from a word for "inspiring fearful awe" to a simpler "very bad." And *awesome* went from "inspiring reverential fearful awe" to a simpler, positive "excellent!"

Terrible/terrific and *awful/awesome* ended up in opposite places but not by randomly and suddenly flipping from one side to the other. They took gradual journeys down different paths that each make sense from one step to the next. *Terrible* and *awful* went from "fear" to more general "negative." *Awesome* took the "reverence" part of the fear and moved in that direction. *Terrific* went from "fear" to associations with size or intensity (a *terrific beast* is large, a *terrific battle* is intense) to more general "positive." The meaning pathway from size or intensity to "positive" is not unusual; it was also traveled by the word *great*. (See "Hey, Large Spender.")

Though certain meaning pathways are common, there is nothing inevitable about the way they will be traveled. *Horrific*, which also came into English in the sixteenth century, did not follow the same road as *terrific*. It continues to mean horrifying. *Formidable*, which also comes from a Latin word for fear, became the modern French way to say "terrific!" but in English only got as far as "scarily impressive."

Fear is a powerful emotion, and people find it useful to tap into that emotion to add some punch to their language. A *hard task* just doesn't sound as important as a *formidable task*. A *loud noise* is just another thing that happens, but a *terrific clamor* deserves a lot more attention. The problem is that over time the punch of fear can wear off.

But people always find a way to bring the punch back. The word *terrifying* still projects the fear that has been drained out of *terrible* and *terrific*. A terrifying bowl of soup is something much less mundane than a terrible or terrific one. Maybe it's full of nuclear waste or poison-tipped darts. Whatever it is, it probably tastes awful, but if the main thing you look for in a hot, trendy new restaurant is originality and excitement, it could be awesome.

Literally Messed Up

How Did *Literally* Get to Mean *Figuratively*?

Sometimes it's not a good idea to take things too literally. If your coach tells you to keep your eye on the ball, it's best not to run over and touch it with your eyeball. If your mom tells you to wait a second, you shouldn't start pestering her again after one second has passed.

To take something literally is to take the words as they are commonly understood and not in their metaphorical sense. The word *literally* literally means "by the letter" or "according to the text," or at least that's how it started out. But in the seventeenth century people began to use *literally* in a slightly extended way, to add urgency to what they wanted to say, to heighten the impact.

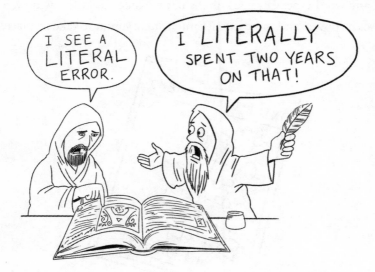

At first the heightened impact came from giving new life to an expression that had been used too often for exaggeration. If you said you had to bite your tongue to keep from saying something, you were using a common expression to show that you really wanted to say whatever you were holding back. If you *literally* had to bite your tongue to keep quiet, meaning your teeth actually clamped down on your tongue, you must have wanted to say your piece that much more. It was a way of upping the emotional stakes. If the emotion led to such a concrete, physical outcome, not just a figure of speech, then you weren't just exaggerating.

Literally proved so useful in this role that it was whisked into the vast and ever-recruiting club of English intensifiers. Intensifiers are words like *very* that add force and intensity. There are a lot of them: *extremely, utterly, totally, super, quite, so, too*—these are just a few. There are so many of them because they have the highest turnover of any word type. Once an intensifier becomes used too widely, it loses its power, and more intense intensifiers sprout to take its place.

Very, one of the older, more established intensifiers, has become pretty bland and boring. But it was new and exciting when it was borrowed from French *verrai* (*vrai* in modern French). It meant the "true," or "one true." It stepped in for tired, older words like *full*, *well*, and *right*, which themselves had previously taken over for Old English *swipe*, meaning "strongly."

The most fertile ground for the replacement of tired, old language is slang. Young speakers constantly freshen the supply of intensity, especially in slang. Words like *thundering*, *stinking*, *plenty*, *lousy with*, and *roaring* give way to *rad*, *way*, *chuffing*, and *wicked*, which give way to *mad*, *crazy*, *hella*, *totes*, and *straight up*. Old words come back from retirement with new credentials; terms that get tired in one community get imported to other communities that haven't exhausted them yet. The field just keeps growing and churning.

Literally was good for livening up metaphors by drawing attention to the imagery in them. Using *literally* to talk about biting your tongue, tearing out your hair, or hitting a wall brought back some pain imagery that may have drained out of those idioms. But soon it didn't matter if you hadn't actually done those things. The intensifying was an end in itself. By the early 1800s *literally* had crossed over and detached from its original sense.

It didn't detach completely, of course. We can still use *literally* to mean "not figuratively." In many ways the development of intensifier *literally* follows the same road as an older intensifier, *really*. *Really* at first meant "in reality" or "in actual fact." But it eventually became an intensifier like *very*. It can still be used both ways. I can ask "Were you really sick?" to mean "in actual fact" if you took the day off and I think you might have played hooky. I can also ask it with the meaning "very," to check in on how bad your symptoms were.

I can also say "Boy, I really had to bite my tongue on that one!" without implying there was any tongue biting in actual fact. *Literally* can work the same way. But *literally* gets a whole lot of criticism that no one ever seems to direct toward *really*.

This criticism started with the usage guides of the early twentieth century. Books like Ambrose Bierce's *Write It Right* in 1909 and H. W. Fowler's *Dictionary of Modern English Usage* from 1926 objected to the nonliteral use of *literally* in the strongest terms. And the attitudes of generations of editors and teachers were shaped by their advice. (See "Blame the Snobs.")

More recently, *literally* critics have argued that the word has come to be used by the confused to mean its opposite, *figuratively*. But that's not really—not in actual fact—what happened. If you replace *literally* with *figuratively* in sentences like "I figuratively had to bite my tongue!" you sound completely strange, as if you assume people don't understand how idioms work, or they've never heard that one before.

Literally did not come to mean *figuratively*. It simply joined the ranks of English intensifiers like *really* and many others before it in a process that's literally run-of-the-mill, really common, and totes normal.

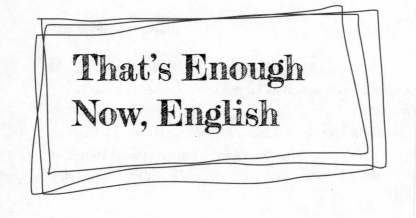

That's Enough Now, English

At the beginning of this book I told you that the weirdness of English wasn't to be found in "mistakes" or nonstandard usage and that "the types of questions I will deal with here are part of fully accepted, unquestionably correct, standard English." I end with the so-called figurative *literally*, which you might argue doesn't fall into that category. But it will someday.

Language will change, and so will our attitudes about it. The whole idea of "fully accepted, unquestionably correct, standard English" is very new in the life of the language and has only had any effect on guiding people's language habits for a short time, a couple hundred years.

That standard has been constantly in flux, and it is overflowing with absurdities. There are many, many more questions I could cover. But this seems like a good place to end. The answer to most "Why does English do this?" questions will be a variation on things we have already seen here: old habits getting reinforced while new habits take over, unnoticeable slow drifts in pronunciation, the practice of extending or borrowing or creating in order to get something useful, reusing materials at hand in new ways, the drive to get more emotional impact, the need to look smart, impress, send social signals, express national pride. It will be because of the old Germanic layer, the French upheaval, the consolidating force of the printing press, the purposeful manipulation done by snobs, or the natural tendencies of our human language endowment.

When language changes, it's never the whole system changing at once. It happens one piece at a time, and the pieces don't coordinate or even communicate with each other while they do this. Contradictions won't be noticed until they're already baked in. All languages have them. English, because of its history, has a lot of them. But that doesn't stop the system from working. It doesn't stop people from learning to use it, from making sense of what doesn't seem to make sense. We don't need to make order out of the chaos; we just need to put it to use.

Acknowledgments

Thank you to Sean, my neighbor, high school buddy, and perfect collaborator. Thank you for being so organized, so fast, so creative, and most of all just "getting" what I was trying to do from the very beginning when we started making whiteboard videos. I handed you heavy, wordy, sometimes hard-to-read stuff, and you handed back just the right visual translation, plus excellent jokes. I am a word person through and through, perhaps too much so, and it's amazing to see my ideas given life through pictures. Also, thanks for all the great suggestions from your own keen ear for English weirdness.

For other great suggestions, I thank Jonah Musto (Why doesn't sew rhyme with new?), Adam Blunt (How come we say how come?), and my daughter, Louisa (Why don't we order a big drink? Why is there an r in Mrs.?)

I couldn't have gotten this project off the ground without the patient ministrations and fierce know-how of my agent, Tina Pohlman, and my editor, Meredith Keffer. There is nothing better for a writer than working with professionals who immediately understand and like your schtick and know what to do with it.

This book would not have happened without the years of work at Mental Floss, where Jason English, Erin McCarthy, and Jessanne Collins helped me discover what people are actually interested in, find the right questions to bring them to my soapbox, and craft an answer that would turn that soapbox into a dance floor at a party we're all invited to.

Thanks to just the right friendly expertise from Peter Sokolowski, to Marc Catchpole for translation, and Alta Price for translation advice and friendship. I couldn't have seen this through without the encouragement of good friends. No one handles my complaining and brings me back to life like Irina Ruvinsky. No one believes in me and sees me in just the way a person would want to be seen, and for forty years at that, like Jenny Hay.

Thanks to Uncle Danny for being my ideal reader and always telling me the truth. Thanks to my mom, Inez, for teaching me to love creative projects and my dad, Larry, for instilling in me such an expansive view of language and the world. Derrick, you make everything else possible. Leo and Louisa, you make everything worthwhile.

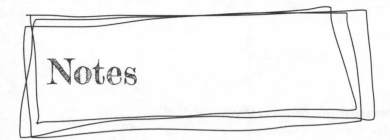

Notes

This book relies heavily on the *Oxford English Dictionary*, which is so much more than what most people think of as a dictionary, a list of words and their definitions. The *Oxford English Dictionary*, the *OED* to those who love it, is a breathtaking feat of scholarship, a more than one-thousand-year history of words, their spellings and pronunciations, their shifts in meaning and grammar roles, their etymologies, and a vast collection of specific examples of how they have been used. It is, as advertised, the "definitive record of the English language." The electronic version (https://www.oed.com) allows for complex searches based on subject, origin, time period, part of speech, and manner of use (e.g., ironic, euphemistic, poetic, etc.). Access to this treasure trove can usually be achieved through a library (my own access came with my Chicago Public Library card). This book could not have been written without it—the dictionary or the public library that made it available to me. May both (ambitious, patient, thorough scholarship, and public libraries) live long and thrive.

p. 3
"compendium of cacography"
"Can any reader name the author"
SSS Newsletter 3, no. 2 (Summer 1986): 17–21. Available online at http://
spellingsociety.org/uploaded_journals/j3-journal.pdf.

"an indictment of the chaos of English spelling"
Journal of the Simplified Spelling Society 17, no. 2 (1994). Available online at http://spellingsociety.org/uploaded_journals/j17-journal.pdf.

p. 4
"rhythm and rhyme may act as fly-wheels"
Gerard N. Trenité, *Drop Your Foreign Accent* (London: Allen & Unwin, 1932).

p. 6
"May it spread fear and dismay"
Charivarius, *Ruize-Rijmen* (Haarlem, the Netherlands: H. D. Tjeenk Willink & Zoon, 1922). Available online at https://www.gutenberg. org/files/56749/56749-h/56749-h.htm#IV_14.

p. 18
There was a brave soldier, a colonel
Steubenville Weekly Herald, October 1, 1880, 1.

p. 30
"Sometimes I think all the English speakers should be committed to an asylum"
There are various versions of this essay that have appeared on message boards and websites and in writing advice books and teaching materials. The source from which all the sentences are drawn is Richard Lederer, *Crazy English: The Ultimate Joy Ride through Our Language* (New York: Pocket Books, 1989).

p. 69
"an ancient and dignified part of our language"
J. B. Greenough and George Lyman Kittredge, *Words and Their Ways in English Speech* (New York: Macmillan, 1901).

p. 87
"this so-called easy language"
Louis Hjelmslev, "Nu kom den dansk-engelske ordbog," *Politiken*, October 8, 1954.

p. 141
The English town of Shrewsbury
"Shrowsbury or Shroosbury—the Results Are In," *Shropshire Star*, June 27, 2015, https://www.shropshirestar.com/news/2015/06/27/ shrowsbury-or-shroosbury-the-results-are-in/.

p. 147
"our grosse tongue ... "

William Barker, *Preface, Addressed to the Earl of Pembroke, of The Bookes of Xenophon Contayning the Discipline, Schole, and Education of Cyrus the Noble Kyng of Persie. Translated Out of Greeke Into Englyshe, by M. Wylliam Barkar*, 1567 (1560?).

p. 148
"many wordes in Latyn ... "

Second Prologue of Hereafter Folowith the boke callyd the Myrroure of Oure Lady very necessary for all relygyous persones, 1530.

p. 148
witcraft

Ralph Lever, *The Arte of reason, rightly termed, witcraft, teaching a perfect way to argue and dispute*, 1573.

p. 178
"orthographic patriotism"

M. Lynne Murphy, *The Prodigal Tongue: The Love-Hate Relationship between American and British English* (New York: Penguin, 2018).

p. 182
a fed-up grammarian wrote up a list

The Appendix Probi. See, for example, Ronald J. Quirk, "The *Appendix Probi* as a Compendium of Popular Latin," *Classical World* 98, no. 4 (2005): 397–409.

p. 193
"I rather wishe Englishmen to content themselves"

John Gerard, *The Herball, or General History of Plantes*, 1597.

p. 194
"The choicest kinds"

John Abercrombie and Thomas Mawe, *Every Man His Own Gardener*, 1767.

Bibliography

Abercrombie, John, and Thomas Mawe. *Every Man His Own Gardener.* 1767.

Barker, William. *Preface, Addressed to the Earl of Pembroke, of the Bookes of Xenophon Contayning the Discipline, Schole, and Education of Cyrus the Noble Kyng of Persie. Translated Out of Greeke into Englyshe, by M. Wylliam Barkar.* 1567 (1560?).

Baugh, Albert Croll, and Thomas Cable. *A History of the English Language.* London: Routledge, 2013.

Bierce, Ambrose. *Write It Right: A Little Blacklist of Literary Faults.* New York: Neale, 1909.

Blake, N. F. *William Caxton and English Literary Culture.* London: Hambledon, 1991.

Charivarius. *Ruize-Rijmen.* Haarlem: H. D. Tjeenk Willink & Zoon, 1922. Available online at https://www.gutenberg.org/files/56749/56749-h/56749-h.htm.

Charivarius and Wim Daniëls. *Is dat goed Nederlands?* The Hague: Sdu Uitgevers, 1998.

Claridge, Claudia. *Hyperbole in English: A Corpus-Based Study of Exaggeration.* Cambridge: Cambridge University Press, 2011.

Claridge, Claudia. *Multi-Word Verbs in Early Modern English: A Corpus-Based Study.* Amsterdam: Rodopi, 2000.

Claridge, Claudia. "The Origins of How Come and What . . . For." In *English Historical Linguistics 2010: Selected Papers from the Sixteenth International Conference on English Historical Linguistics (ICEHL 16), Pécs, 23–27 August 2010,* 177–196. Amsterdam: John Benjamins, 2012.

Crystal, David. *Spell It Out: The Curious, Enthralling and Extraordinary Story of English Spelling.* New York: St. Martin's Press, 2012.

Daunay, Marie-Christine, and Jules Janick. "History and Iconography of Eggplant." *Chronica Horticulturae* 47 (2007): 16–22.

Dekeyser, Xavier. "Some Considerations on Voicing with Special Reference to Spirants in English and Dutch: A Diachronic-Contrastive Approach." In *Recent Developments in Historical Phonology*, 99–122. Berlin: Mouton de Gruyter, 1978.

Durkin, Philip. *Borrowed Words: A History of Loanwords in English.* Oxford: Oxford University Press, 2014.

Erickson, Amy Louise. "Mistresses and Marriage: Or, a Short History of the Mrs." In *History Workshop Journal* 78 (2014): 39–57.

Fowler, Henry Watson. *A Dictionary of Modern English Usage.* Oxford: Clarendon, 1926.

Gerard, John. *The Herball, or General History of Plantes.* 1597.

Gisborne, Nikolas. *The Event Structure of Perception Verbs.* Oxford: Oxford University Press, 2010.

Greenough, J. B, and George Lyman Kittredge. *Words and Their Ways in English Speech.* New York: Macmillan, 1901.

Hjelmslev, Louis. "Nu kom den dansk-engelske ordbog." *Politiken,* October 8, 1954.

Hoeksema, Jack. "On the Natural History of Negative Polarity Items." *Linguistic Analysis* 38, no. 1 (2012): 3–33.

Hogg, Richard, and David Denison. *A History of the English Language.* Cambridge: Cambridge University Press, 2006.

Horobin, Simon. *Does Spelling Matter?* Oxford: Oxford University Press, 2014.

Hotta, Ryuichi. "A Phonological Motivation behind the Diatonic Stress Shift in Modern English." In *Historical Linguistics 2013: Selected Papers from the 21st International Conference on Historical Linguistics, Oslo, 5–9 August 2013*, 3–18. Amsterdam: John Benjamins, 2015.

Ito, Rika, and Sali Tagliamonte. "Well Weird, Right Dodgy, Very Strange, Really Cool: Layering and Recycling in English Intensifiers." *Language in Society* 32, no. 2 (2003): 257–279.

Jones, Richard Foster. *The Triumph of the English Language: A Survey of Opinions Concerning the Vernacular from the Introduction of Printing to the Restoration.* Stanford, CA: Stanford University Press, 1953.

Kreidler, Charles W. "Stress Differentiation in Sets of English Words." *WORD* 38, no. 2 (August 1987): 99–125. https://doi.org/10.1080/00437956.1987.11435883.

Laing, Margaret. "The Early Middle English Scribe." In *English Historical Linguistics 2006: Selected Papers from the Fourteenth International Conference on English Historical Linguistics (ICEHL 14), Bergamo, 21–25 August 2006*, 1–44. Amsterdam: John Benjamins, 2008.

Lederer, Richard. *Crazy English: The Ultimate Joy Ride through Our Language*. New York: Pocket Books, 1989.

Lowth, Robert. *A Short Introduction to English Grammar*. 1762.

Minkova, Donka. "Constraint Ranking in Middle English Stress-Shifting." *English Language and Linguistics* 1, no. 1 (1997): 135–175.

Mugglestone, Lynda. *The Oxford History of English*. Oxford: Oxford University Press, 2013.

Murphy, M. Lynne. *The Prodigal Tongue: The Love-Hate Relationship between American and British English*. New York: Penguin, 2018.

Orel, Vladimir E. *A Handbook of Germanic Etymology*. Leiden Brill, 2003.

Orr, John. *Old French and Modern English Idiom*. Oxford: Blackwell, 1962.

Ostler, Rosemarie. *Founding Grammars: How Early America's War over Words Shaped Today's Language*. New York: St. Martin's, 2015.

Phillips, Betty. *Word Frequency and Lexical Diffusion*. New York: Palgrave Macmillan, 2006.

Prins, A. A. *French Influence in English Phrasing*. Leiden: Universitaire Pers Leiden, 1952.

Buyssens, Eric. "Prins. French Influence in English Phrasing," 1953.

Quirk, Ronald J. "The Appendix Probi as a Compendium of Popular Latin." *Classical World* 98, no. 4 (2005): 397–409.

Schlüter, Julia. "To Dare To or Not To: Is Auxiliarization Reversible?" In *Formal Evidence in Grammaticalization Research*. Edited by An Van Linden, Jean-Christophe Verstraete, and Kristin Davidse, 289–326. Amstedam: John Benjamins, 2010.

Schreier, Daniel. "Initial Cluster Reduction in English." In *Consonant Change in English Worldwide*, 56–125. London: Palgrave Macmillan, 2005.

Second prologue of Hereafter Folowith the boke callyd the Myrroure of Oure Lady very necessary for all relygyous persones. Richard Fawkes, 1530.

Sherman, Donald. "Noun-Verb Stress Alternation: An Example of the Lexical Diffusion of Sound Change in English." *Linguistics* 13, no. 159 (1975): 43–72.

Swift, Jonathan. *A Proposal for Correcting, Improving and Ascertaining the English Tongue: In a Letter to the Most Honourable Robert, Earl of Oxford and Mortimer, Lord High Treasurer of Great Britain.* Benj. Tooke, 1712.

Taeymans, Martine. "DARE and NEED in British and American Present-Day English." *New Perspectives on English Historical Linguistics: Selected Papers from 12 ICEHL, Glasgow, 21–26 August 2002* vol. 1, *Syntax and Morphology*, 215–227. Amsterdam: John Benjamins, 2004.

Tagliamonte, Sali, and Rika Ito. "Think Really Different: Continuity and Specialization in the English Dual Form Adverbs." *Journal of Sociolinguistics* 6, no. 2 (2002): 236–266.

Thim, Stefan. *Phrasal Verbs: The English Verb-Particle Construction and Its History.* Topics in English Linguistics 78. Berlin: Walter de Gruyter, 2012.

Toupin, Fabienne. "About Plural Morphology and Game Animals: From Old English to Present-Day English." *Lexis*, May 13, 2015. https://doi.org/10.4000/lexis.964.

Trenité, Gerard N. *Drop Your Foreign Accent.* London: Allen & Unwin, 1932.

Upward, Christopher, and George Davidson. *The History of English Spelling.* Malden, MA: John Wiley & Sons, 2011.

Viberg, Ake. "Swedish Verbs of Perception from a Typological and Contrastive Perspective." In *Languages and Cultures in Contrast and Comparison*, 123–172. Amsterdam: John Benjamins., 2008.

Villalta, Gema Maíz. "The Formation of Old English Adverbs: Structural Description and Functional Explanation." *Miscelánea: A Journal of English and American Studies* 41 (2010): 37–57.

Wheale, Nigel. *Writing and Society: Literacy, Print, and Politics in Britain, 1590–1660.* London: Routledge, 1999.

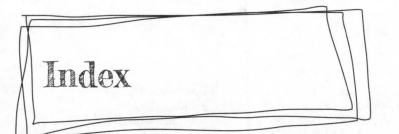

Index